LOVE

prosperity

FAMILY

gratitude

Faith

opportunity

My Life

Full of Blessings

Success

COUNTRY

Career

FRIENDSHIP

GOD

Happiness

By Andrew Valrosa Jr.

My Life Full of Blessings

By Andrew Valrosa Jr.

My Life Full of Blessings
All Rights Reserved.
Copyright © 2022 Andrew Valrosa Jr.
v1.0

The opinions expressed in this manuscript are solely the opinions of the author and do not represent the opinions or thoughts of the publisher. The author has represented and warranted full ownership and/or legal right to publish all the materials in this book.

This book may not be reproduced, transmitted, or stored in whole or in part by any means, including graphic, electronic, or mechanical without the express written consent of the publisher except in the case of brief quotations embodied in critical articles and reviews.

Outskirts Press, Inc.
http://www.outskirtspress.com

ISBN: 978-1-9772-5789-5

Cover Photo © 2022 Andrew Valrosa Jr.. All rights reserved - used with permission.

Outskirts Press and the "OP" logo are trademarks belonging to Outskirts Press, Inc.

PRINTED IN THE UNITED STATES OF AMERICA

My Life Full of Blessings

Chapters

1. Growing up in The Bronx   pg. 1
2. In the Navy   pg. 27
3. Under the Sea   pg. 60
4. Life After the Navy   pg. 66
5. A Career at Boeing   pg. 85
6. My Other Life   pg. 107
7. A Growing Family   pg. 122
8. Friends, Old and New   pg. 135

Foreword

In my life, I have been blessed with the many people God has placed before me. Sometimes I may wonder why or wish certain things had not happened. I believe things happen for a reason, though you may not understand why, since you don't have access to His big plan. Some facts are missing, either because it was so long ago I can't remember or too painful to remember. With that said, over the years as I shared my many blessings and life events with people, there were those that were amazed and said to me that I needed to write a book. I usually laughed in response…."who would buy or read a book about me and my life"? Well now that I am retired and have more time on hand, I decided to give this a shot. If it never gets published it may remain as a memoir for someone, but who really knows. Anyway, here it is and thank you to those that influenced me to do this.

1

Growing up in The Bronx

My family had left Harlem, where many Italian immigrants lived in the 30s through the 50s. We moved to The Bronx, 975 E. 178 Street, on the 5th floor of a walkup apartment building. My earliest memories began when I was 2 years and 10 months old, and I had the pleasure to overnight at Montefiore Hospital where I got my tonsils out. I still have vivid memories of being on the operating room table and the anesthesiologist placing the mask (ether) over my face to knock me out. I remember waking up in a crib screaming, probably because I had my first sore throat. I remember taking a taxi home with my mother, and when we arrived my father was in the kitchen with my sister teaching her how to play Chinese checkers. Now today, over 60 yrs. later, I understand why I still fear the thought of going to a hospital or receiving anesthesia.

When I was between 1 and 2, my parents were concerned because I would not talk. Instead of speaking, if I wanted something, I would point and whistle. My grandmother and others started calling me Mr. Fischietto, which means the whistler. I am told it used to upset me because I thought they were calling me Mr. Fishcakes. They took me to the doctor who told them there was nothing wrong with me and I would talk when I felt like it.

Moving on, after my parents divorced when I was around 3 and a half, my mother, sister and I stayed in the same apartment.

I remember the parquet wood floors and my mother on her hands and knees with the steel wool and shellac to keep them looking good. We played but always cleaned up our toys on our own when we were finished. There was no maid service in our home. We played in the stairwells with our slinky, or in the courtyard between the 2 buildings. I remember the signs on all the buildings that stated "FALLOUT SHELTER", but of course did not know what they really meant. Every day at noon the air raid sirens would go off. We were told it was just a time check to let everyone know it was noon. Little did we know or would we have understood that we were on the brink of a nuclear attack from Cuba. Of course New York City was an easy target from Havana.

School

Kindergarten started in '61 for me, at PS6, 1000 E Tremont Ave. As a 6 year old, I could already get dressed, tie my own shoes, and knew how to tell time (on an analog clock with the 2 hands). School was just 2 blocks away, and my sister and I were taught how to walk there and back home again, since my mother had to work. Denise was 18 months older than I was. The house key was on a shoelace around my neck so I wouldn't lose it. It amazes me nowadays when my friends will not allow their Junior High or even High School kids to walk to school in their quiet suburbia neighborhoods. I had a colleague that would not let his 12th grade daughter walk to school if she missed the bus. They lived half a mile from school. I once told him, do you realize in a few months your daughter will graduate and still not have experienced walking to school or work! They say it's "different" now as to imply it's now much more dangerous. I guess they don't remember the pictures on the Borden Milk Containers.

Our training to become street smart started at a young age, i.e. how to cross the street even when there was no stop light, don't stop to talk to strangers, and of course, don't accept candy from strangers. The main thing that is different now is the spoiling and coddling of children and letting them grow up inexperienced in life with false expectations of security.

The following year we transferred to Saint Thomas Aquinas, which was probably a 6 block walk from home. Mom walked us to school for the first few days or so, then we were on our own. We only attended for the first semester and then during Christmas we moved to the Morris Park area of The Bronx, where I lived until I left for the Navy. I attended St Francis Xavier on Haight Avenue. This was a 16 block walk up Morris Park Avenue, or we could take the city bus. The bus fare was 15 cents for a single ride, or 50 cents for a weekly bus pass with unlimited rides. For perspective, a slice of pizza was also 15 cents and a candy bar was a nickel. So whenever I was given 30 cents to take the bus somewhere, the dilemma was should I walk and buy 6 candy bars? Heck if it was only a mile or so, I chose the candy bars.

Starting in 2nd grade we then transferred to St. Dominic's school, which was in the neighborhood, only 3 blocks away. Tuition for Catholic school was not free. My mother paid $15 per month per student, so $30 a month for my sister and me. To give you perspective, we paid $110 a month rent at the time so tuition was 25% of the cost of our housing. In today's dollars if you are paying $1,600 a month rent then add an additional $400 a month for tuition not including inflation. Mom worked 3 jobs starting with her regular 40 hour week in the office. She would get home on the subway just before 6pm. Sometimes I would meet her and walk home together. After dinner, a few nights a week she was a coat checker at a restaurant/catering hall. She also brought home typing to do for law offices, etc. That is why it was common for kids to start getting jobs when we were 12 years old, because there was no extra money for bicycles and other important toys we may want. People were very reluctant to go on welfare, or "Home Relief" as it was called. Italian immigrants were too proud to ask the government for relief. They just worked harder and sacrificed more for necessities and did without the luxuries. Only one of my uncles owned a house when I was a kid. Uncle Mike bought his house when he was in his mid-30s, because that's how long it took to save money for a down payment. Nowadays, if you cannot buy a house when you are 25 you are a victim of some sort and somehow society has denied you of something and dealt you a bad hand. My father didn't own a house until he was in his late 30s.

Mrs. Graziano was my 2nd grade teacher. She seemed really old at the time, probably in her 50s. She earned our attention because she told us about the "paddywacking machine" that she had at home if we misbehaved. She lived just 1 block from school and the first time I got in trouble and had to go home with her to do a punish lesson after class. Man! I did not want to go into that room where the paddywacking machine was! She cut me slack and just had me write my punish lesson out 100 times. I was quite the good boy after that. Of course nowadays she would have gotten fired and brought up on charges and sent to prison. I remember once when my mother and I were in the principal's office and my mother stood there and told Mother Josephine and I quote, "you have my permission to do whatever it takes to keep him in line". WOW, imagine a parent saying that now?

Over the years there were many winter days that we walked to school in snow that was half way up to our knees with our rubber boots on, which we left just inside the classroom door.

Snowball fights in the school yard during lunch were part of the norm. In the better weather we played now banned games, such as dodge ball, ringalario, and Johnny Rides the Pony. The losers would have to "moon up" which meant they would kneel against a wall on all 4s, with their butt up and then the winners got to throw the ball at the target. These games would never be allowed in today's society because there were definite winners and losers and would most likely hurt someone's feeling. There were no participation awards or trophies back then. If you won, the others would congratulate you and if you lost it motivated you to play harder next time. At the end of the day everybody went home happy and still friends.

Most of my years at St. Dominic's I had nuns as teachers. I spent many afternoons after class walking to the convent after school let out to do my punish lessons. They knew I had to be home before dinner so probably I would stay for an hour from around 3:30 to 4:30. This only interfered with my after class play time and there was no way I was telling my mother I spent another afternoon in the Convent. Punish lessons usually involved saying the Rosary, or writing "I must not xxxxx" some countless amount of times. I actually was a smart student that may have been a little bored. I did typically make the Gold Honor Roll regularly which was for those that had a 95 or better average in all classes. Math and Science were always my favorite subjects with History at the bottom of the list. I never understood why the school had a goal that everyone be able to read at 2 grades above their level. Even then the logical me, which often got mistaken for sass, would say... If I am in 4th grade why do I need to read like a 6th grader? Well later in life this is something that you come to understand.

I became an altar boy when I was in about 4th grade. I had to memorize the entire mass in Latin. When I told Fr. Anthony I was ready to take the test to be an altar boy, he told me hold off because Vatican 2 just changed the mass to English. Well you may think this was easier but actually no. I memorized all the words in Latin but did not know what they meant, nor the translation, so I had to start all over again.

After school activities consisting of boxing lessons and also the youth club were held in the gym. The youth club had all equipment such as the ropes (my favorite) that went up to the ceiling about 30 feet, chinning bars and floor exercises. At the end of each night we had a relay race. I think this was probably a once a week activity, as were the boxing lessons. Our Lady of Solace had Sea Cadets and our school, St. Dominic's had Marine Cadets, which I also joined. We got our first experience at military discipline, marching, shoe shining and my favorite, was in the summer months when we went to the wooded park for war games. Of course, since we were all street wise it was not a burden on your parents for you to participate because you could walk to and from school in the evening with no problem.

There were 2 classes of each grade level in the school. There were only about 5 or 6 lay teachers in the school. I did not have one until 6th grade. We heard a new teacher named Mr. O'Hara was going to be our teacher. None of us knew what to expect because we could not ask the previous class since he just arrived. Well, the first thing we noticed was that they had separated the girls into one class, and the boys into our class. The other obvious change was that the teacher's desk was not in the center front of the room. It was in the back corner behind row 6, furthest from the door which was in the front at row 1. Well after the bell rang -no teacher yet-, so we did what kids do, start carrying on and getting loud. I'm sure it was a setup and he was waiting outside for the appropriate time to make his grand entry. In comes Mr. O'Hara, running across the front of the classroom, then making a left turn after row 6, running down the aisle and leaping onto his desk like Superman. There we sat in silent amazement and he stood looking at us, with this ¼" thick 18" ruler in his hand. "I am Mr. O'Hara and this is Herman. First row, up against the front wall". Then he proceeded to give each and every one of us a really hard whack with Herman. He wanted to let us know what we would be in for.

Well, initially we revolted against this type of treatment with leaving him nasty notes, wishing that he would be drafted, sent to Vietnam and gets his head blown off, and other pleasantries. This was in 1967. I even got in trouble for attempting to give him 4 flats. Eight nails wedged on either side of all 4 tires so if he went forward or backward... 4 flats. Someone ratted me out so his tires were spared but my ass was not. It took us a few months to accept him and actually our relationship grew into a big brother type of relationship.

Mr. O'Hara took us to the park (Trojan Field) to play football after class, and other activities he participated with us in. He turned out to be a great teacher, and in fact, in 8th grade we had him again and were all very pleased, except that they now integrated the girls back into our class. The girls were not as happy as us as since they heard about his strictness. When the time came they got equal treatment as the boys. Herman had no problem placing his sting right through their wool plaid skirts.

6th grade c.1967

WOW... as I am writing this I just found out about Mr. O'Hara. New York Post 9/14/2019 Headline: Child sex abuse victim nabbed his own tormentor, became FBI agent. Investigators believed O'Hara, who died in 2000, had as many as 200 victims. He was first reported in the 1960s in Hewlett, Long Island, when the Boy Scouts created a **"perversion file"** on O'Hara

Upon completion of 8th grade we took a test for acceptance into Catholic High School. You applied for up to 4 schools for acceptance and based on your test scores and grades you were notified of your acceptance. I was accepted at all the 4 schools I had put in for, St Raymond, Mount St. Michael, Cardinal Spellman and Cardinal Hayes, in spite of having no intention of attending Catholic High School. I was ok with Religion as a separate subject but was tired of it being part of math and every other subject. I then also applied to Bronx High School of Science and Peter Stuyvesant High School and was accepted at both. These are among the top High Schools in the country. Well I found the average student at Science was too much of a Poindexter nerd for me, not my type. I was a street kid not a nerd, in spite of having the grades and ability to get in. So I registered for Stuyvesant.

Operated by the New York City Department of Education, these specialized schools offered tuition-free accelerated academics to city residents. Stuyvesant was a college-preparatory high school. Many world-class leaders, technologists, and magnates graduated from Stuyvesant High School. It is one of only six secondary schools worldwide that can claim to have educated four or more Nobel laureates. Stuyvesant was located in lower Manhattan, which meant I would have to take the subway to school. Not a problem since I was taught how to ride public transportation at the age of 8, unlike the coddled kids we raise today.

Then the summer before starting 9th grade, I decided to move to live with my father. I felt the need to have a male father figure in my life. Dad lived in an upper middle class neighborhood in Syosset, Long Island. This created a problem since I would then have to take the Long Island Railroad to Penn Station in Manhattan and then the subway down to 15th Street. That would have been one heck of a commute, so I ended up going to the local school in Syosset. Syosset had an excellent school system. It was there that I met my BFF Lori Webber who has stayed in close touch through thick and thin over the years. Her parents were awesome as was her older brother too. He was a Green Beret that served in Vietnam. A hero and victim of Agent Orange.

Syosset High School was in a great setting just about 2 or 3 miles from dad's home. The school bus came to pick us up, unless I overslept, which meant I was walking to school that day. On Fridays after chores such as mowing the lawn, I would make my way back to the Bronx to stay with my mother for the weekend. I took the Long Island Railroad to Jamaica, Queens where I got on the Q44 bus to The Bronx West Farms, then the 26 bus up Morris Park Avenue. Not a big deal for a 9th grader back then since we were raised to be street smart, as I mentioned before.

High School dances were usually fun. Spellman had great dances and since my sister was 2 grades ahead of me, I knew the "older" girls in her class so I always had someone to flirt and dance with. Usually we went as a group of guys, picked up some beer and headed to the dance. St. Catherine's had good dances too. Back in those days there were all live rock and roll bands at the dances.

Unfortunately after 2 years of living with dad, I decided it was not what I had hoped for and moved back to The Bronx with mom. I then went back to Stuyvesant and tried to re-register but they would not accept me. I only had 2 years of school left and they required that you completed at least 3 of your 4 years there to get their piece of paper upon graduation. I can understand them not wanting someone to go to Joe Blow High School and then transfer in for their last semester and get a diploma from Stuyvesant.

So, I then registered at Christopher Columbus High School, the local Joe Blow High School. I attended school for a week or so until the school was shut down due to racial riots. Several hundred kids from the neighborhood and outside the neighborhood would assemble in the street to fight. Over a dozen gangs existed then and since we all had bus and train passes there were members from the South Bronx and Harlem coming to participate. Police were stationed at the Pelham Parkway train station to deter gang members from getting off the trains. Obviously this was not what I was looking for in a High School experience, so I ended up just working more instead and quit going to school.

Some of the older guys on the block were our role models growing up. One in particular, Burger, had just come home from the army. We talked and we decided the military would be a good option, but I remember him saying, Air Force or Navy. So he took me to the Navy recruiter and sat with me as I took my entrance exam and negotiated my conditions to enlist, a guaranteed school. I was not 17 yet so I had to wait for my birthday with my mother's consent to actually sign and join. I was sworn in and off to boot camp by the end of January.

The Neighborhood

We lived in a working class neighborhood, 90% Italian immigrants and 1st generation mostly. The local businesses were mostly Italian owned, delis, dry cleaners, pizzerias, butcher shops, bakeries, etc. The immigrants were comfortable living there because they did not feel intimidated that they didn't speak English, because most of the workers spoke Italian in all the stores. These were close knit ethnic neighborhoods where everyone knew everyone. We did not have drones, video games, Xboxes, cell phones or laptops growing up. We had friends, and we often made our own toys or things to play with. An old broom stick and a pink ball (Spalding) and we were good to go. Stickball was often played in the street with the bases marked on the ground with chalk. Hide and seek, Ringalario and Johnny rides a Pony were all games we played that required nothing but our own bodies.

Johnny rides a pony

Johnny rides a pony has 2 teams. The first team, the pony, is the lower ones bent over holding the teammate in front of them. The other team, one at a time, runs and jumps on the "pony" and keeps moving forward. The object is for the lower team to not break the chain and once all of the other team has mounted, they yell "Johnny rides a pony 1 2 3, 1 2 3, Johnny rides a pony 1 2 3". If they succeeded this far and the chain was not broken, they win.

We ate cupcakes, white bread, real butter and bacon. We drank Kool-Aid made with real white sugar. And we weren't overweight! Why? Because we were always outside running and playing.... That's why! We would leave home and go out to play and as long as we were home before the streetlights came on, it was ok.

There were many ethnic neighborhoods growing up in NYC. Morris Park was predominantly Italian. As a result you got to experience your cultural heritage on a daily basis. While diversity is good to learn other cultures, learning where you came from should be a first.

I hate the expression "It takes a village", maybe because of its origin of fame. But growing up in an Italian neighborhood was like that. If you screwed up and a neighbor caught you, there was a good chance he would take you to tell your parents about it. This was not ratting someone out. This was very different than being a rat fink which was very frowned upon in the Italian culture. This was about neighbors and friends helping each other, especially if you were being raised by a single mom who could not be around all the time. Sometimes just the thought of your neighbor bringing you to your mom or having a talk with you was enough to make you think twice next time.

We helped each other doing things which also served as a teaching/learning experience. I was changing the oil in my mother's car by the time I was 12. I changed mufflers for her and for neighbors. Pattyboy's father was a mechanic so he had the jacks and tools and was always happy to teach/explain how to do it. Tune ups, changing spark plugs and points, rotor and distributor cap… no problem for me or any of my other friends on the block by age 14. Most of our parents were just getting by so if there was something we wanted, we learned to work for it. Think about that next time your teenage kid says he/she "needs" a new iPhone 20 or whatever number they are up to. Some of my younger friends have told me "you don't understand". "We grew up poor so we want our kids to have everything they want". Well they are right, I don't understand because our parents didn't have a pot to pee in and wouldn't have spoiled us if they did. They worked 2 or 3 jobs to provide the necessities but also ensured we understood the value of a dollar and how to work for one. This meme says it all about today's youth…

> **Only in America do you find a kid wearing $150 tennis shoes, drinking a $5 cup of coffee, typing on his $1000 cell phone complaining on social media that he is oppressed and that capitalism has failed him!**

I used to love to go fishing. My cousins Mary and Richard lived on City Island in a waterfront apartment building. They had no kids so I used to hang out there a lot even overnight when school was out. I would get my fishing pole and tackle box and walk about half mile or so to catch the #12 bus at Pelham Parkway which went to City Island. Jack's bait and tackle shop was at the start of the island so I would get off there and buy a box of worms for about a buck a dozen.

Then I would walk 16 blocks to my cousin's place. The parking lot was at the water's edge with a fence along it. There would be half a dozen of the regular locals out there fishing. With a worm on the hook, I would cast out and wait. Flounder, Black Fish and an occasional eel, were always the dinner for the four of us.

On a typical hot summer day in the Bronx, someone would go get the big wrench so we could open the fire hydrant to cool off. This was a very common activity in the 60s. Of course the people driving cars down the street would have to close their windows as they passed. We would get a tin can and take both ends out of it and use it to direct the water like a water cannon.

When I was about 10 yrs. old, somebody decided that my sister and I needed to take accordion lessons. My maternal grandfather played accordion in spite of having a missing ring finger on his right hand. And he played very well. So we had to schlep our accordions to music school twice a week. This meant schlepping them 2 blocks to White Plains Road, catch the bus to Gleason Avenue, which was about a mile and a half or two away. I hated carrying that accordion. I did not last long with it, though my sister did continue and got pretty good. I was more interested in a guitar. After all, this was the era of rock and roll, and Hendrix and Clapton did not play the accordion. I bought an old acoustic guitar and sanded it down and refinished it. My friends Timmy and Dennis, who were both probably 5 yrs older than me, were both great guitarists so I had good teachers. I eventually wanted an electric guitar, so I found a Univox Les Paul knockoff with real Humbucking pickups. It was a great ax with great action. Once again I was never good but we had a lot of fun hanging out on the block jamming. Next door neighbors Brian and Duke joined in. Brian died (RIP) when someone fell asleep smoking and burned the place down. Duke (RIP) O.D. on heroin. When I was in 6th grade I attended 3 funerals of older friends that O.D. on heroin. That was enough to remove any interest in me trying it. Heroin was very popular in the late 60s and early 70s. It was good that I got out of town.

Food

Food played a very important role in our lives growing up. Most of our parents and certainly our grandparents remembered the Great Depression. I think this was a factor in how they used food to reward and celebrate. It was commonplace to sit the life insurance man down when he came for his monthly payment, to a plate of whatever was for dinner that night. Also, to invite your teacher over for dinner a few times each year. Unfortunately we were taught to eat 5 times more than we really needed but what the heck, it tasted so good it was fun! Everyday meals at home were almost a routine. Thursday was always pasta. Sunday was also always pasta. Friday was typically pizza and lentils or some kind of fish, since we didn't eat meat on Friday back then. We ate Roasted chicken with potatoes on another day. There were no Chicken Nuggets or McAnything. You ate what was put in front of you as you got a lecture about the kids starving in Biafra if you didn't finish it.

Holidays were exceptional. Christmas eve for example, The Italian culture celebrated the "Feast of Seven Fishes", except in our house, as many others, it was more like the Feast of 20 Fishes. It was a 3 hour sit down experience. Then after dinner all the men would go for a walk around the block while the women cleaned up and got the espresso going and the desserts ready to serve. On Thanksgiving, we first had the homemade Manicotti with meat balls and sausage, and then the turkey and American sides came out. Easter was another special homemade pasta, either Lasagna, Manicotti, Cavatelli or Gnocchi to name a few. After the pasta and meatballs and braciole, the traditional leg of lamb came out. Of course there would also be an assortment of vegetables to go with it. Salad was eaten last after all the other food.

There were all the great Italian delis every few blocks. When you walked in, the homemade sausages would be hanging with the cheeses to dry. The aroma filled the air and before you walked out you were sure to have a sudden appetite. Living away from NYC and the great delis, I do miss some of the foods that now are special treats that you get on occasion instead of every day. Soppressata is different from salami. It is made using a much courser grind of pork and fat and usually some white wine and can have hot pepper or not. It is then stuffed into intestine casings and hung to cure for about 45 days or so.

Nothing better than some Soppressata with a few chunks of cheese and some Italian bread and a bottle of wine! The perfect lunch.

And let's not forget the pastries and Italian Ice in the summer. Pastries to die for. Cannoli, Sfogliatelle and Napoleons are among my favorites.

Cannoli **Sfogliatella**

Napoleon

Nothing better than a sfogliatella warmed up in the toaster oven!

Of course there is nothing like New York Pizza! Hear that my friends in Chicago! I was lucky to not have developed an allergy to wheat until I was in my 50s. That gave me half a century to enjoy all the wonderful Italian baked foods one could want!

Growing up, a slice of pizza, which was 1/8th of an 18" pie, was 15 cents. The pizza was amazing and we did not Americanize it with 10 different toppings on it. Usually it was only 1 or 2 toppings selected from pepperoni, mushrooms, anchovies or sausage. Two slices and a soda was a meal.

Let's not forget the dirty water hotdogs. They got their name because the vendor with the cart just kept adding more and more hotdogs into the same water as they were sold. Sauerkraut or onions? Two with mustard and onions (sautéed w tomato) please.

Or as an alternative you could always get a knish. A knish is a mixture of mashed potatoes with some onion, wrapped in dough, and either baked or fried.

If you haven't had a knish from a pushcart in Manhattan, Brooklyn, Queens, The Bronx or Staten Island, then I don't know where as a New Yorker you've been living. Cut in half and put some mustard in the center and indulge!

Working in the 60s

We learned to work for whatever toys we wanted. Washing and waxing a car for $10 was a regular opportunity during the summer months. At 12 yrs. old you could get a paper route. I had a good route with 75 customers, mostly in apartment buildings with elevators. These were the fastest ones to deliver to. Once a week we "collected". It was 65 cents for the week of the N.Y. Post papers, Monday through Saturday. If you got 75 cents and they told you to keep the change that was a decent tip. If they gave you a dollar and told you to keep the change, that customer got whatever special service they wanted for their paper, i.e. under the door mat, in the milk box, ring the bell and hand it to them. A 75 customer paper route could yield you up to $14 a week for your labor. We typically carried the papers in a shopping wagon. In the winter when it snowed, the papers got put on your sleigh and pulled. That was how I was able to save for my first 10 speed bicycle. It cost $60 back then around 1967.

There was always some kind of work to be had if you were willing to work. At age 10, I started shining shoes. I had a box that my father made for me that held all the polish, brushes, buffing rags, etc. in it. It had a shoe rest on the top, for the customer to place his foot onto as you did your magic. The price then was 15 cents for a shine. Popular places to solicit were train stations at the end of the workday, catching businessmen coming home, in front of a large department stores, or on a block that had lots of people traffic. I remember once shining Mayor Lindsey's shoes. His bodyguard gave me a dollar and told me to keep the change. I thought I was rich.

One summer, Ralph got me a job working in construction for Moe. I think we were paid $10 for the day, which was BIG bucks then when minimum wage was $1.00 per hour. But let me assure you we earned every dollar. I got assigned to help the brick layers. My job was to hand mix mortar, shovel it into a wheelbarrow and run it over to the bricklayers. Then back and forth, repeated for the rest of the day.

When I was around 15 or so, Tony from across the street, had a moving truck. He did furniture deliveries for local appliance and furniture stores. I don't remember how much I was paid but once again this was no easy job. N.Y.C. had a majority of walk up apartment buildings back then, so bringing a refrigerator or sofa bed up the stairs to the 5th floor was common. I gained valuable knowledge on how to move large pieces of furniture through doorways and tight turns that I still use even today, when I move or help friends move. I continued doing this until my 17th birthday when I left New York to do my duty to God and Country.

2

In the Navy

Off to Boot Camp

Eight days after my 17th birthday, I was at Whitehall Street getting sworn in. It was the one time that I was actually in control of the Navy and not vice versa. I met 2 guys from Arthur Avenue in The Bronx there also waiting to be sworn in. The Commander handed us orders, told us to go upstairs and get sworn in. Vinny and Frenchie got orders to Orlando FL for boot camp. My orders read Great Lakes, IL. It was January and Orlando sure sounded much better than Great Lakes. I asked the Commander if he could change my orders to Orlando to be with my buddies. He said no. So I took a chance and said F*** it, I'm not signing and threw the papers down and walked out. In 15 seconds there was a Commander running down Whitehall Street yelling to me, "OK, OK!" So we all got sworn in and were on our way to the airport to fly to Orlando. We checked in, were given a blanket and pillow and brought to our barracks. This was an open bay room with bunk beds on both sides from one end to the other. It was lights out, so time to try to sleep.

The next morning after waking up, our Company Commander came in to introduce himself to us, and to give us our first lesson. Evidently one of the recruits tried to commit suicide that first night. Heck we didn't even have to do anything yet. He attempted to cut his wrists and failed, so we received a lesson on the proper method to cut your wrists most effectively.

I won't go into a lot of details on Boot Camp, since we have all either been there or have seen enough movies. In addition to all the physical training and marching, there were many other valuable life experiences such as, how to scrub the floor with a toothbrush, how to do laundry by wearing your clothes into the shower, then finish scrubbing them on the table before hanging them on the roof to dry. After the first week, we all had an assignment to write to our mothers and apologize to them for being such pains in the ass while growing up. You were taught the value and meaning of being a team member. One day when we got back to the barracks, we found all of our clothes on the ground at the bottom of the stairs. One of our brother recruits had left his locker in other than perfect condition so everyone's locker was emptied and dumped outside. There were other lessons on being part of a team. For example, if one recruit screwed up everyone got to pay the price and do the pushups and jumping jacks and squats. This served two purposes. It taught each of us that the entire team is affected by the action or lack of action of each of its members, and also the failed individual got a special lesson of peer pressure, if not immediately, then usually that evening after lights out.

For those that did not know how to swim, they got pulled out of our company for a week or so and placed in a special company where they spent their days at the pool. I was surprised how many people my age did not know how to swim. For whatever reason they were mostly from the south. You had to pass swimming and water survival skills in order to graduate boot camp. This included techniques such as removing your pants once in the pool, tying knots in the bottom of the legs and then filling them with air to act as a floatation device. Similarly, your shirt and also even your dixie cup white hat could be used to hold air. I had to jump off of a 40' high platform into the pool to teach you to cross your legs before entering the water, to prevent you from becoming a soprano from the impact of the water or potential debris.

After about the first few weeks in, you took a series of tests to help determine what "rating" or field of training you would go into after boot camp. When I joined I was guaranteed DS, Data Systems Technician, but upon going over my educational history with the counselor it became apparent that I had not graduated high school. He told me since I fraudulently enlisted they were going to discharge me. I assured him the only reason I lied about graduating high school was at the advice of the recruiter. Well they let me stay in but I lost my guaranteed school. So I applied for 4 other electronic type ratings. I was then assigned to be an AE, Aviation Electrician's Mate.

Heading to "A" school

AEA School was in Jacksonville FL. One of the first things I needed when I got there was a car. I had saved $200 and went down to the Navy Federal Credit Union, joined and applied for a $400 loan so I could buy a 1966 GTO that I saw for sale. I sat down with the loan officer and she approved it on the spot. $600 was a great price because the owner had attempted to rebuild the engine not having a clue. I was able to drive it to the auto hobby shop on base where I immediately pulled the engine, completely tore it apart and put it back together correctly. A 389 with 2 deuces, 4 on the floor. Wish I still had that car now. I drove that care to New York over July 4th weekend without a starter. Yes we did crazy things when we were young. I didn't have the money to buy one at that time, so, whenever I stopped for gas I left it running. If I stopped to eat I parked in the uphill section of the parking lot so I could push start it when I was ready to leave. I did get a new starter to put in when I got to N.Y.

Jax was a fun place for a young sailor. The beach was awesome and you were allowed to drive your car on it. Don't party too hardy and fall asleep at low tide if you parked too close to the water. Back then they had drive-thru package stores that sold liquor. You could drive thru and buy a beer or a drink, and legally drink it while driving, as long as you were not intoxicated. No open container law back then. The enlisted club on base was usually packed on the weekends. Live bands were the norm in the early 70s. Most of my buddies were either black or Spanish, and also the best dancers on the floor. It was hanging out with them that introduced me to dancing fast which was a great way to score points with the ladies.

Daytona Beach was a short drive from Jax, under 2 hours. Like Jax Beach, you could drive on the sand and party right there beside your car. Daytona was really happening with young people on the weekends, even when it wasn't spring break. There were clubs galore and parties all night long. If you couldn't have a good time in Daytona there was something seriously wrong with you.

One day after a hard evening of partying, I woke up to get to class. I went outside to the parking lot and could not find my car, so I just walked to class. When school was finished that afternoon I went to security to report my car missing. The security guard drove me all over the base looking for it, to no avail. He thought it was funny that I was out drinking the night before and "lost my car". A few days later I got pulled out of class to go to the office where I had an important call. "Hello… this is Joe". I asked Joe who. "Joe from the FBI, we found your car". I guess since the car was stolen on Federal property the FBI got involved. Well he came to the base to pick me up. My car was in a hotel parking lot about 5 miles from the base, undamaged. Someone took it for a joy ride. I thought it may have been my roommate Kelly since the keys were used. I never knew and will never know.

When you buy candy bars from the vending machines in FL, you watch carefully what drops down with the candy. Never leave a bottle of Coke open overnight. You will be amazed what you can catch in it. Works better than a Roach Motel.

School was 22 weeks long, class was 8 hours a day, 5 days a week. We studied basic airplane fundamentals as well as electrical and electronic theories and circuit analysis, including vacuum tubes, (for you old timers that remember what they were), followed by transistor theory. As a side activity I joined the Drill Team. I got to learn some of those fancy rifle twirling moves we have seen in various videos. I seem to remember enjoying being part of that team.

Upon graduation, there were 25 sets of orders placed on the table and 25 of us were lined up in the order of our final grades. I was 2nd highest grade in the class so I got 2nd choice of orders out of the 25 that were placed there. There were many sets of orders for new P3 squadrons that were forming in Brunswick Maine. That sounded boring to this 17 year old that wanted to be where the action was, so I grabbed the set that would most likely get me to visit Southeast Asia. Many others were happy to take orders to Brunswick because it would be safe. The ironic part of this was that several months later, while floating in the Tonkin Gulf off the coast of North Vietnam, I read in the Stars and Stripes newspaper about a P3 crash in the icy Atlantic off Brunswick Maine. You never know when your time is up, even during a routine non-combat training exercise.

Next stop…. NAS Whidbey Island WA

Transferring from Jax to Whidbey Island where my squadron was due to deploy soon, I drove my GTO to New York for some leave (vacation) and then continued on to WA. This was my first time driving cross country. Being from an Italian family, they ensured I had all the necessities in case I broke down in the Rockies, and it took a month to find me. I had enough food to feed an army, blankets and water. The trip was mostly non eventful for the most part except for 2 things. I got stopped in PA for doing 95 in a 65. The cop told me they were letting everyone go that was doing under 85. So I took my ticket and continued on.

Then, when I was passing through Salt Lake City, my clutch went out. I found a gas station but it was a Saturday night and the stores would not be open till Monday morning. I had to check in by Sunday or I would be UA (Unauthorized Absence or AWOL). I explained my situation to the owner of the station, and he let me keep my car there. I then proceeded to hitchhike to Whidbey. I was lucky I got picked up by a hippy couple who was driving to Alaska, so they took me all the way to Seattle. They felt compassion for me and decided they would drive me all the way to the base on Whidbey. I really lucked out!

I got checked into my new squadron okay, worked the week, bought a new clutch, packed my bags the next weekend and hitch hiked back to Salt Lake to get my car. The gas station owner let me do the work there and it only took an hour or so to drop the transmission and change the clutch. Then I was on the road again, starting my 13 hour 900 mile drive from Salt Lake to Whidbey. I got back in time to report for work on Monday morning. WOW what an adventure thinking about this 48 years later as I write.

When I first saw my orders to NAS Whidbey Island, I said where the F*** is that? I looked at a map and decided that I would just have to go to Seattle on the weekends for action and to party. Well as it turned out I almost never went to Seattle. The area offered everything I was looking for. Night life was great, since there were at least 5 clubs in town with live bands. Only problem was drinking age was 21 and I was still 17. The enlisted club allowed drinking 3.2% beer if you were under 21, so that was the place to hang out. They also had live bands and since the club was actually off base in housing area, you did not need a pass to get on base to go to it. As a result all women were guests of the management and did not need a sponsor to sign them in. The place was packed. College students came down from Bellingham and other girls came from surrounding towns, since there was no other place they could go to being under 21. Only active duty military could drink 3.2% beer being under 21 at the club, but they were still allowed in. Most of the bands were awesome and we even had the occasional well known band. Once The Drifters played. Well it was common to have house parties when the bars closed at 2am, so that night I gave a piece of paper to The Drifters with my address and told them to come over at quitting time. Unexpectedly, they announced "the party is at Andy's follow us". I shared a 14x70 single wide trailer at the time. I called my roommate to give him a heads-up. There were so many people there we carried out any furniture that was not a sofa or chair and put them in the carport. They sang acapella and we partied our asses off. One neighbor came over to ask us to hold it down and when she saw it was The Drifters, she went home and got her husband. They joined us in their PJs. Cleanup the next day was interesting as we found beer bottles and joints everywhere.

Outdoor life had almost everything you could want. The skiing was good. The slopes often opened by Thanksgiving, with real snow, not the manmade ice particles in the baby hills of the Appalachians. Hunting far exceeded that of back east. There was Deer, elk, bird (which I never got into), bear hunting. I did enjoy deer and elk hunting.

Deception Pass

Fishing for salmon in the 70s was great. I typically caught a limit (usually 3 fish) almost every time out, unlike nowadays when you're lucky if you catch anything that they allow you to keep.

My first boat was a 1956 18' Reinell carvel-planked wood boat with a 75 HP outboard. It had a little cuddy cabin with a porta potty and an ice box. When I got it the owner was going to just bury it in their yard as a decoration. I may have given them $50 for it, I don't remember. I towed the boat home and took it off the trailer, setting it on bails of rags. I bought a Craftsman 4" x 24" belt sander (which I still have 45 yrs. later) and sanded it down to the bare wood, repainted the hull, and refinished all the wood. I put in all new electrical wiring, lights and speakers for my stereo, and made new cushions for the bunk.

Working swing shift allowed me plenty of daytime to work on it each day. While it didn't look totally new, it was fully restored close to new. Many fish were caught on that boat and many nights slept on it. Her name was Aquarius.

Dad and me

Kow Korner had the best burgers in town. There was no McDonalds, Burger King or Wendy's. We didn't need them.

Attack Squadron 95, Green Lizards

Newly formed, VA-95 was my first squadron to be assigned to. This was the third **VA-95** established April 1, 1972 and reclaiming the original "Green Lizards" name. The first VA-95 was established in 1943, as an **Attack Squadron** of the U.S. Navy. We were getting ready to deploy on a West Pac (Western Pacific) cruise. We would deploy on the U.S.S. Coral Sea, CVA-43 and make our way over to South East Asia. The ship was homeported in Alameda just outside of San Francisco, so we flew from NAS Whidbey to Alameda. Checking in onboard was quite overwhelming. This was a floating city with 5,000 crew members onboard and all the comforts of home, lol. Our work shop was off the hangar deck so it was easy to find, but finding our berthing compartment took some practice, as did to the mess hall and other places. Every compartment is identified with a number which clearly identifies what deck it is on, whether it is on the port or starboard side, and how far forward or aft it was. The next morning we were going to be shipping out and sailing west. First stop would be Pearl Harbor. It is a 10 day cruise to Pearl, plenty of time to learn my way around the ship. First day out to sea we recovered all the squadron's airplanes as they flew onboard to join us. We flew A6A Intruders and KA6D tanker version of an A6. On the way to Pearl, we would get all the planes into ship-shape and ready for our mission.

Our 2 nights in Pearl were a bit disappointing to me. I was envisioning big white sandy beaches with coconut trees and hula girls. In reality it was high rise hotels built on the sand at the water's edge. I called it Los Angeles on the water. However, the night life was good, with lots of clubs and, of course, the International Marketplace was loaded with shopping and restaurants.

Visiting the Arizona Memorial was very moving and really made you think about what you could be in for as you headed back to the ship that night getting ready to get underway. It would be about a 2 week cruise till we arrive in Subic Bay, our last stop before heading to Yankee Station (coast of North Vietnam).

Crossing the Pacific

Being at sea was a new experience for me. One thing we always looked forward to was Mail Call. I was always assured of receiving a letter from my BFF from High School, Lori. The envelope was sprayed with Intimate perfume which she wore. Can you imagine what the mail bag smelled like with a few hundred of these letters in them? Of course, the other anticipated mail was from my mother…. A box with goodies in it like pepperoni, provolone, and other yummy things from the deli. My locker was always a popular place when it got opened.

Anytime you were at sea, an E2, (Early warning aircraft) was airborne to protect the fleet. The E-2 Hawkeye is the Navy's all-weather, carrier-based tactical battle management airborne early warning, command and control aircraft. The E-2 is a twin engine, five crewmember, high-wing turboprop aircraft with a 24-foot diameter radar rotodome attached to the upper fuselage. The Lockheed Martin AN/APS-145 radar can track more than 2,000 targets and control the interception of 40 hostile targets. One radar sweep covers six million cubic miles, so we can see them coming and react expeditiously.

E2 Hawkeye

We always had an F4 Phantom, the Alert 5, on the catapult fully armed, ready to launch and be airborne within 5 minutes. The alarms went off… LAUNCH THE ALERT 5, LAUNCH THE ALERT 5… THIS IS NOT A DRILL. Time to get your butt on the flight deck and get that Phantom in the air. The Russian Bear was heading toward our ship. After the Alert 5 was launched, we launched 2 more Phantoms. Several minutes later, we watched as the Bear flew over our ship being nosey, with a Phantom tucked under each of its wings and another on its ass. If those Bomb bay doors even cracked open it would have had half dozen sidewinder missiles up its ass in a heartbeat. What was the excitement for the day, I later learned to be a regular event with our Russian friends while crossing the Pacific.

We got to see new lifeforms crossing the Pacific.

Flying fish were a daily observance.

Then one day we caught a sea bat. It was down on the hangar deck in a large cardboard box. There was a hole in the box so you could bend over and get a glimpse of this rare finding. As you bent over to look through the hole in the box, someone would whack your ass with a bat and yell SEABAT. I don't know if these activities are allowed in today's politically correct Navy.

I did get to complete my GED while on cruise, opening the door for me to go to college.

GED presented by C.O. CDR (Zip) Zirbel

My first port – Subic Bay, Philippines

I was very excited to see my first overseas port, as we arrived in Subic Bay, Philippine Islands. My shipmates gave me a quick lesson on how to be street smart in P.I. First, have nothing in your back pockets. Be aware of when 3 kids surround you, because they are going for your pockets and can also get into your socks for your cigarettes. Next lesson was how to say, "Kiss my ass" in Tagalog. This was used when they kept stopping you saying, "Hey Joe, give me a coin".

As you go through the main gate leaving the base to go to town, you walk across a bridge, aka Shit River Bridge. This was the name because it had so much raw sewage in it. Rumor had it that, if you ever fell in, you would have to get some ungodly number of shots. In the meantime, the river always had dugout canoes in it with young kids and a young honey asking you to throw them coins. If it went into the water they would dive down to get it.

Shit River Bridge with the Main Gate in the background

Nightlife in Olongapo was among some of the best for a young sailor. Very inexpensive, a beer was about 15 cents. You could have a nice meal for 2 dollars. You could have many other things that I won't go into details here, for very little money. Magsaysay Drive, the main drag, was wall to wall clubs with occasional hotels.

Magsaysay 1972 before Marcos martial law

Magsaysay 1974 after paving

    The clubs all had live bands that were very talented. The clubs also employed hostesses, whose jobs were to entertain you and keep you in that bar so you kept buying drinks. They sat with you, flirted and played with you, danced with you and, if they liked you, they may even take you home with them at closing time. One thing to understand is that for many of these working girls, their job was not for a life of luxury. It was for their survival and that of their families. They were not to be looked down upon as tramps but just as a working girl.

Most of the bar girls dreamed of marrying an American sailor and getting a ticket to the United States. In fact, base authorities said that more than 15 such marriages a week were the rule.

Their job was to keep you company, keep you happy, keep you buying drinks!

Pick your choice!

Martial law was in effect so there was a curfew from midnight till 5am. Nobody was allowed on the streets. You could however, be on your front porch area if you had a fence enclosing it from the sidewalk. This was good in a way because the bars all closed at 11:30, so you didn't have to stay out all night. By 11:15 you knew if you needed to start walking back to the base or if you had a place to stay for the night. Martial law also made it safer. If a local got caught with any weapon, even a knife, they were going to jail. And if they had it out waving it around, they would be shot.

Once on my birthday the girls bought me drinks all night. I must have gotten hammered because the next morning I woke up in the bar (which was closed) lying on top of a table with a white tablecloth over me and flowers all around me, like a corpse. I guess they laid me out the night before, so all the customers to pay their respects to me. LOL. Mama-san, of course, took off my jewelry and money to ensure nobody stole anything.

The most common mode of transportation was the tricycle. It cost you 1 Peso (almost 7 pesos to a dollar) for a ride home or back to the base in the morning, unless they thought you were not street wise and then they would try to take advantage of you.

The food was also quite yummy in P.I. Casual snacks could be bought from the street cart vendor. For 1 peso you could get a skewer of BBQ monkey meat (maybe pork, who knows), or a piece of chicken, or squid on the stick, or chicken feet. It sounds strange but it actually was all pretty good.

Monkey meat on stick

Of course if you went to a restaurant you could get all of the classic Filipino dishes.

Clothing was another great deal in P.I. I wore nothing but tailor-made pants and shirts. A nice tailor-made shirt would cost around $2 and a pair of pants maybe $3.

Back to sea

Typical line period at sea back then was around 30 days or so, followed by about 5 days in port somewhere. Except it seemed like every time we were due to pull back into Subic, we got extended on the line because the U.S.S. Ranger was broke down, again, in Subic and could not relieve us. Nothing better than breaking down in port and having to stay longer. One time did a 64 day line period, which was unheard of back then. We did not have "beer days" and, if you got caught with any kind of alcohol, it was 30 days in the brig. So trust me, after 64 days of working 16-20 hrs. per day, tempers were quite short.

Full load of MK-82 500 lb. bombs

So now we were heading to Yankee Station. During Vietnam, Combat Pay was $65 per month, and Flight Deck hazardous duty pay was $55 per month, if you worked on the flight deck during flight operations. The biggest financial advantage of being in the combat zone was that your entire pay was tax free. Oh and let's not forget free mail! When you sent a letter home you just wrote Free Mail up in the corner where you normally would put your stamp. An E2 in 1972 earned $320.70 per month base pay. An E3 earned $333.60. WOW what a huge increase $12.90 a month raise. So an E2 in Vietnam with combat pay made a whopping $385.70 per month!

Our squadron provided support for Operation End Sweep, the clearing of mine fields along the coast of North Vietnam in Haiphong harbor and other coastal and inland waters between February and July 1973.

I loved working on the flight deck. The view was great, the danger was exciting. Described as the world's most dangerous working environment, [1] the flight deck of an aircraft carrier is extreme. In the small span of the flight deck aircraft take off, land and taxi, ordinance is moved around – and all this is done 24 hours a day, outdoors, in every sort of weather possible. Aircraft carrier flight deck crews must be professionals to know their way around and to get the job done without being injured or killed in the process.

Carrier Job description: The main mission of an aircraft carrier is to move air power around the world so that it can be on location when it is needed always. Although the aircraft and pilots are an important part of the aircraft carrier crew – they cannot operate without the help of the flight deck men and women. The flight deck crews of an aircraft carrier perform all duties necessary for the aircraft to safely operate from the carrier. There are several types of flight deck jobs, and flight deck crews wear colored jerseys to distinguish their role.

The flight deck of an aircraft carrier is probably the busiest deck on earth. In the space of 350 yards X 80 yards, dozens of aircraft can be taking off, landing, taxiing and being refueled and armed. All this is also done outdoors, 24 hours a day and in the middle of the ocean. Aircraft carrier flight deck crews must have

---

[1] https://dangerousjobsguide.com/

their heads on a swivel at all times, always on the lookout for aircraft moving about, starting their engines and other vehicles on the flight deck. The color code helps greatly.

Death and injury can come in many ways on an aircraft carrier flight deck – befitting its title as the world's most dangerous workplace. Flight deck crews can fall overboard (either blown off by engine exhaust or simply fall off), be sucked into engine intakes, get hit by aircraft or other vehicles, struck by propellers and rotors or be caught up in moving parts of aircraft. Another danger is fire and explosions. Ordinance can ignite or overheat and explode, and fire is also a major concern.

When on deployment, flight deck crews can expect to work 12-22 hours a day, depending on the operations going on each day. Work is done 7 days a week. This job demands complete devotion. Everyone on the flight deck helped out with various tasks. Even though I was an Electronics type, we all helped hump these bombs up.

MK-83 1,000 lb. bomb

The iconic early example of the *Intruder*'s ability to hit targets any time was when two A-6As attacked a North Vietnamese power plant during a particularly dark and stormy night. The *Intruder*s dropped 26 Mark 82 500 pound bombs on the target, but the damage they caused convinced those on the ground that B-52s had carried out the attack instead.

Of the 84 Grumman A-6 "Intruders" lost to all causes during the war, 10 were shot down by surface to air missiles (SAM's), 2 were shot down by MiG's, 16 were lost to operational causes, and 56 were lost to conventional ground fire and AAA. Most U.S. Marine Corps Grumman A-6 "Intruders" were shore-based in South Vietnam at Chu Lai and Da Nang. The last Grumman A-6 "Intruder" to be lost during the war was from Squadron VA-35, flown by LTs C. M. Graf and S. H. Hatfield, from the carrier "USS America". They were shot down by ground fire on 24 January 1973 while providing close air support. The airmen ejected and were rescued by a Navy helicopter. Twenty U.S. Navy aircraft carriers rotated through the waters of Southeast Asia, providing air-strikes, from the early 1960s through the early 1970s. Nine of those carriers lost Grumman A-6 "Intruders": "USS Constellation" lost 11, "USS Ranger" lost 8, "USS Coral Sea" lost 6, "USS Midway" lost 2, "USS Independence" lost 4, "USS Kitty Hawk" lost 14, "USS Saratoga" lost 3, "USS Enterprise" lost 8, and "USS America" lost 2.

Other ports of call during this deployment included Hawaii, Subic Bay, PI, Manila, PI, Hong Kong, and Sasebo, Japan. We were supposed to also go to Yokosuka Japan after leaving Sasebo, but since the Japanese government asked us to leave the country when in Sasebo, we had to skip that port. The reason for getting thrown out of Sasebo was due to racial riots. Some months prior to our arrival the USS Kitty Hawk had some severe racial riots. This gave the people of Sasebo a bad taste for American sailors. When our ship arrived and we went to town, there were signs on the bars that stated "Welcome Whites from CVA-43". Well you can imagine the firestorm that this started as it fueled the already ticking time bomb of tensions from the civil rights movement at home combined with the already tense situation onboard. After 2 days we were asked to leave the country, so we headed back to Subic. According to a congressional report, sleeping sailors were pulled from their racks and beaten with fists and chains, dogging wrenches, metal pipes, fire extinguisher nozzles and broom handles. Fights regularly would break out in the mess decks for the next several weeks until tensions eased a bit.

In October 1973, at the end of our deployment, every day I would go up to the flight deck and see the sun rising over the bow. Well one morning I went up and saw the sun over the stern. It became immediately obvious that we turned around and were not heading home. Moments later the skipper announced what I had suspected. Where we were going was classified but if we kept sailing west that would put us in the Indian Ocean. Hours later, the world was on the verge of a nuclear confrontation. DEFCON (or Defense Condition) III, the highest state of armed forces readiness for peacetime conditions, was declared in the name of President Nixon. Any plane capable was loaded with live nukes. What we trained for was becoming reality before us. This was really scary. Most of America never had a clue this happened but it was the first time we were placed on DEFCON level III since the Cuban Missile Crisis. According to documents declassified in 2016, the move to DEFCON 3 was motivated by CIA reports indicating that the Soviet Union had sent a ship to Egypt carrying nuclear weapons along with two other amphibious vessels. Soviet troops never landed, although the ship supposedly transporting nuclear weapons did arrive in Egypt. Further details are unavailable and remain classified. After a couple of days of sweating we went back to DEFCON IV and headed home. We later learned that this was the Yom Kippur War, also called the Ramadan War, and Arab-Israeli war of October 1973.

We returned to home port San Francisco on November 8th 1973, and the air wing returned back to their bases, which for our squadron was NAS Whidbey. Upon returning home it was typical to have a 30 day stand down, where there was no flight operations and squadrons were manned at an absolute minimum level. I did not take leave until Christmas time to go back to New York and spend time with the family, as I needed some time to adjust after the past deployment. I usually spent the first half of my leave period going around to say hello to everyone, then the 2nd half going around saying goodbye to everyone. I gained at least 10 lbs. in that 30 days at home with my mother and grandmother cooking. After just a couple of trips home I realized that most of my friends had not changed, and were still just hanging out on the stoop doing the same thing as a year or two ago, and really not achieving. I also realized that there were other places to live in this great country besides New York.

In April 1974 I reenlisted for 6 more years under the STAR (Selective Training And Reenlistment) Program, where I was guaranteed to go to B school (advanced electronics). I was a 3rd Class Petty Officer (E4) at the time. It would be another year before I actually sign up for school. This now brought my total commitment to 8 yrs., 2 mo. and 1 day, which brings me to point out a possible bad decision in my Navy career. Before I joined I was asked if I wanted a congressional appointment to Annapolis. At that time as a 17 yr. old, I could not even begin to imagine making an 8+ year commitment when I wasn't even sure I would survive 4. As it turned out I ended up serving over 8, and getting out without a degree and then having to go back to college to get one. But oh well, who knows what could have happened and how the course of my life may have changed. More than likely I would not have ended up with the career and friends I had at Boeing for 29 yrs., and definitely would not have had the experience I got in construction and as a Journeyman electrician which played a major role in me building our first home. More on that later.

My friend Bob and I dated 2 girls that lived up in Bellingham, about an hour from the base. We would spend the weekends up there, drive up Friday after work and back to the base Monday morning. We took turns driving each week. Well one day it was Bob's turn and half way up he was getting tired so he asked me if I would drive. Bob had a 59 Vette... "oh hell ya I'll drive". Well the next week I sold my GTO and bought a 68 Stingray. I built the engine, 327 fuely, sanded the entire car down and did a really nice lacquer paint job at the auto hobby shop on base. It was very, very sexy, with tee tops, dark blue metallic with dark blue velvet interior. And it was very fast. I can't believe the only picture I have of it is one in black and white.

I drove that Vette from Whidbey to New York at least 2 or 3 times. I also drove it to Tennessee when I got stationed there to go to school. My BFF Lori still tells the story of when I was in New York and we drove down to the Feast of San Gennaro in Little Italy with it. There was no place to park so I parked on the sidewalk, safe from it getting scratched.

Our 2nd Deployment, December 5th, 1974...

Though I'm not sure how much I remember, we did spend Christmas at sea, steaming between Pearl and Subic Bay. In checking the ship's Deck Logs, it appeared we had flight operations that day which means I worked. Must have been so much fun that I just cannot remember.

I do however remember one day of operations on the flight deck, when the plane captain signaled for the pilot to start his starboard engine. Moments later there was a call for a troubleshooter and AO Keller, knowing that the starboard engine was started, approached the back of the plane on the port side, just aft of the exhaust. Well to all of our surprise, the pilot had inadvertently started the port engine. When Keller popped his head up it sent him flying over the side. I immediately signaled the pilot to shut down the port engine. He looked at me not understanding why so I climbed up the boarding ladder, grabbed the throttles and shut them down. I then climbed down and ran to the side where Keller went over. There he was completely blown over the side, hanging from his fingers holding on to the net (horizontal chain link fencing) on the edge of the port side of the ship.

I immediately jumped into the net and grabbed him by the belt on his pants. The net, which was a bit old and rusted, started to feel like it was giving. Just then a CPO, rather large guy, was about to jump in to help but I was afraid the net would break so they found a skinny guy to jump in. We pulled Keller back onboard.

The only recognition I got for my heroic deed was from Keller when we pulled into port, the beers kept coming, but then again, it was enough knowing that I potentially saved a shipmate.

Aircraft from VA-95 participated in Operation Frequent Wind, the evacuation of American personnel from Saigon, when it fell to the North Vietnamese April 30, 1975. The squadron provided armed escort flights over the Saigon area for protection of the helicopters conducting the evacuation.

Shortly after that I left the ship just before it headed to Perth, Australia. That would have been an excellent port from what I was told, but I was heading to Millington, TN, just north of Memphis, to go to AVIC-7 school. That was the advanced school I was guaranteed as part of my re-enlistment.

Millington TN

I had a great 6 months in Tennessee. I had a part time job bouncing at a country western bar. The band played the same songs in the same order every weekend, but there were lots of ladies. I connected with the bartender and we dated for several months. I lived off base in a little town north of Millington called Munford, Hick city USA.

On July 4th weekend, I went camping with a friend to a park in Heber Springs, AK. The lake there was amazing. In fact, it was my first experience with SCUBA.

A guy was diving by himself and let me hang on to him and share air. This was the day after seeing Jaws in the theatre. Well, a trout about 10" long swam by my mask and I thought it was Jaws and I was going to die. LOL. It was funny after the fact, but not during.

That evening I heard a noise and some people running around my tent. So I popped out with my flashlight in my left hand and my pistol in my right. I shined the light on him and ordered him, "stop or I'll blow your head off". Well, as I approached, the closer I got the shinier his badge got. It was the sheriff and his deputy. They took my gun but did not arrest me. I explained that I thought I was going to be robbed. I guess they were chasing some druggies who then got away.

A few weeks later I had to go to court in Heber Springs. I wore my dress blue uniform. The judge asked how I pleaded, and I said not guilty, not even sure what the charges were, maybe for having a gun in the park? Anyway, I told him what had happened and he understood why I didn't trust anyone, being that I was from The Bronx. He asked the sheriff if he ran the numbers of my gun. The sheriff said no so he ran off to do that. Then it became very casual with the Judge. Asked me what I did in the Navy and asked me what my various ribbons were. Then he asked me where I had traveled, and asked what it was like in the Philippines. I had a feeling he knew but wanted to see what I would say. Well the sheriff came back and told him the gun was clean, registered to me in TN. The judge then said "I'm going to give you the leniency all servicemen deserve...... NOT GUILTY". I thanked him, got my gun back and got out of Arkansas. Every time I hear the song 'I shot the sheriff' it brings back memories.

I don't think I ever saw it rain like in Tennessee. I remember once going to Overton Square in Memphis to party. Keep in mind this was way before GPS existed. I remembered turning where there was a big field and cow pasture on some backwoods road. Well going home that night, I could not find that cow pasture. I kept making U turns going back and forth looking for the field with the cows. Then it dawned on me.... I don't remember seeing a lake. And I realized the cow pasture became a lake while I was downtown that night. I learned to park uphill at the barracks parking lot the first time I found my Vette in water up to the seats. After opening the door and draining it to the threshold level, I found the plugs in the floor which I removed to drain the water. Thank God it was summer and hot, so leaving the doors and windows open eventually dried it out.

One morning I woke up and started driving to work. Just a quarter of a mile down from my house there was an empty lot where a house stood the night before. I thought... where the heck did that house go? Well I later found out there was a tornado that passed by overnight and touched down just on that one house, then lifted up and went on. At my place we didn't even hear any wind. Crazy! I don't know what that person did to piss off Someone that controls tornados, but it evidently lifted that house right off the foundation and took it to God only knows where.

Back to Whidbey, then out to sea

After graduation, I received orders to go back to Whidbey Island, which was just fine with me. I checked into Attack Squadron 145, VA-145. The following spring, 1976, we deployed onboard the U.S.S. Ranger, CVA-61. I was looking forward to this since, as you remember, when I was onboard the Coral Sea, the Ranger was always broken down in port in Subic. I figured this was going to be a fun cruise with lots of in port time. As it turned out, the boat never broke down.

Four *Forrestal*-class supercarriers built for the United States Navy in the 1950s. Although all four ships of the class were completed with angled decks, *Ranger* had the distinction of being the first US carrier built from the beginning as an angled-deck ship. Commissioned in 1957, she served extensively in the Pacific, especially the Vietnam War, for which she earned 13 battle stars. On 28 May 1976, while on deployment, helicopter crews from HS-4 aboard Ranger, detachments from HC-3 on Camden, Mars and White Plains, and helicopters from Naval Air Station Cubi Point, Republic of the Philippines. They all assisted in Philippine disaster relief efforts in the flood ravaged areas of central Luzon. Over 1,900 people were evacuated, more than 370,000 pounds (170,000 kg) of relief supplies and 9,340 US gallons (35,400 l) of fuel were provided by Navy and Air Force helicopters.

Next port....Singapore

Independence Day, July 4th 1976, was a big party in Singapore. There are many American Expats in Singapore. I'm sure the presence of the 7th fleet pulling in added to it, as they set up a huge party at some park. There was a BBQ, live music and beverages. I remember it being a great day for the 200 year anniversary of our country. Singapore was hands down the cleanest country I had ever visited. A bit extreme in some regards, such as, you cannot buy chewing gum in the country because they did not want it on their sidewalks or other places. No Playboy or Hustler magazines were allowed. We were briefed to leave any of that stuff onboard.

Bugis Street was the place to go at night. Bugis Street was renowned internationally from the 1950s to the 1980s for its nightly gathering of prostitutes, transvestites and transsexuals, a phenomenon that made it one of Singapore's most notable destinations for foreign visitors during that period.

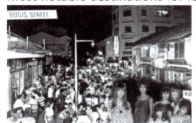 

Bugis Street then

Bugis Street now

All the restaurants and bars put tables outside as they closed the street to vehicles. Food, music, drink, and girls (better check the package because half were trans). I always found it interesting that a country with such strict laws about smut magazines and chewing gum allowed this.

Crossing the Equator

After leaving Singapore, on July 7, 1976, we headed south of the Equator. The Shellback Initiation is a ritual that dates back at least 400 years in Western seafaring. The ceremony observes a mariner's transformation from a slimy Pollywog, a seaman who hasn't crossed the equator, to a trusty Shellback, also called a Son of Neptune. It was a way for sailors to be tested for their seaworthiness. When a ship crosses the equator, King Neptune comes aboard to exercise authority over his domain and to judge charges brought against Pollywogs that they are only posing as sailors and haven't paid proper homage to the god of the sea.

High ranking members of the crew and those who have been Shellbacks the longest dress up in elaborate costumes and each play the part of King Neptune's court. King Neptune and his royal court: his queen, Davy Jones, the royal baby, and other dignitaries, arrive to the ship the evening prior to the equator crossing. Pollywogs receive a subpoena from Davy Jones to stand before the court the next day and answer to charges brought against them by the Shellbacks. After breakfast, which is made too spicy for the Pollywogs to eat, the accused appear before King Neptune, who sits in judgment. The polywogs perform a variety of activities which might involve wearing their clothes inside out or backwards and crawling across the deck through objectionable debris, often the uneatable breakfast that was served to the Pollywogs. It would often be the 'garbage shoot', which is a fabric made tunnel about 50 feet or so long, filled with very ripe left over food and scraps, baking in the sun.

The worse thing was when someone in front of you stopped half way through to puke, adding to the debris.

While crawling around on your hands and knees, the Shellbacks would be showing you what a length of fire hose feels like across your ass.

 Next, the Pollywogs kneel before the King and kiss the royal baby's belly, which is covered in grease. There was also the Royal Dentist and others that you can only imagine.

Lastly, the Pollywogs take a royal bath in a pool of sea water before being declared Shellbacks. Covered in all kinds of things that you dare not bring back to your berthing compartment, you either got hosed down with the firehoses or just stripped and threw your clothes over the side. Upon completion, you would receive your certificates, which you could proudly hang on the wall at home.

I am sure that IF this tradition is still allowed now, with females onboard and the political correctness in the military, it is certainly toned down quite a bit. I find it sad to see how much Naval tradition has been lost due to political correctness.

Tattoos after a day of drinking

The only thing that kept me from getting a tattoo was I could never decide what I wanted to live with for the rest of my life. My friend Garrel Powers, AE-2, thought he would never make AE-1 after trying repeatedly. So once, while we were out drinking when the ship was in port, he got an AE-2 crow tattooed on his left arm, because he figured he would be that forever. Well don't you know next the year he passed the test and got promoted. Not sure if he ever got the 3rd chevron added to his tattoo.

Although this happened a year after I got out, I wanted to mention this shipmate and friend of mine from VA-145. Garrel was a great guy who had an unfortunate accident in 1981 onboard the U.S.S. Kitty Hawk. Following a collision between an F-14 and an A-7, the F-14 crew ejected and the A-7 was recovered and landed taking the barricade on the flight deck. Something snapped on the barricade and took Garrel's life. RIP shipmate.

Last tour Tactical Electronic Warfare Squadron 129 VAQ-129

VAQ-129 was the "rag" outfit for the EA6B Prowlers. The rag is the training squadron for the flight crews. The Prowler was a 4 seat aircraft, with a pilot and 3 ECMOs (Electronic Countermeasures Officers).

The pod hanging below the wing on the outboard is an ECM pod. You can see the propeller in the front which drives a generator to produce the power needed for the electronics and jamming equipment contained within. You can hang up to 5 of these pods on each aircraft.

This was a shore duty tour which meant no deployments overseas. I served as the AE shop supervisor for about a year, then my last year I moved over to Quality Assurance and was 2nd shift supervisor. In QA I got to signoff inspections on a variety of jobs including engine replacements, flight control replacements and other special repairs that required a 2nd inspection after the CDI (collateral duty inspector) signed off.

It was common when spare parts became hard to get, you would just rob them from one plane that was down for multiple other issues. That plane was called a hangar queen. Sometimes it may take a couple of months to get it all back together again, and a great amount of work and inspections required. About a month and a half before I was due to be discharged, we put our hangar queen back together. I did sign off multiple items on that plane and then on the evening of February 26th, 1980, EA-6B Prowler BuNo. 158031/'NJ-910' of VAQ-129 crashed. Destroyed when crashed into Puget Sound short of runway during night landing approach to NAS Whidbey Island, Washington, all three crewmembers - Lt Commander Richard Smith, Lt (JG) William Readman and 1st Lt Thomas Mushyn (ECMO) - were killed.

This was very traumatic and as QA supervisor, I immediately had to secure all maintenance records and lock them up. I was also responsible for a work detail that went to the beach off the runway. We were there all night till the sun came up, gathering and loading 2 flatbed tractor trailers, looking for anything that washed up to shore. This included aircraft parts and body parts. I will leave this at that. It sucked bad. All the airplane parts recovered including those recovered by Navy divers, were brought back to the hanger where they attempted to lay them out and experts try to determine the cause of the crash.

I was afraid of being placed on legal hold until they finished the investigation as to the cause of the accident. It was determined not to be related to any repairs or airplane failures so my discharge was not held up. I was Honorably Discharged April 1, 1980.

3

Under the Sea

While attached to Attack Squadron 145 in the mid '70s, I found a new interest…. SCUBA. My brother in Christ, Pete, was a certified diver, so one day when in port in Subic, we went out to Grande Island, a resort island owned by the navy, and got into the water. Pete gave me a briefing on some underwater physiology and the dos and don'ts, and we were ready to get wet. It was amazing and I was immediately hooked. Visibility there is over 100 feet and the ocean is littered with sea life. When we were done, we surfaced about a ¼ mile off shore. Pete laid back and said he had a cramp and could not swim. He made me tow him back to shore, where he then laughed, because his cramp had magically disappeared. He told me he just wanted to be sure that I would be a good dive buddy, and able to carry his ass back to shore in case of emergency.

So it was time to sign up for scuba lessons. There was a dive shop in Subic called SEAUS dive shop (South East Asia Underwater Specialties). It was owned by a former Navy SEAL who was medically retired after losing his hearing in an underwater explosion. All of his fellow instructors and safety divers were active SEALS, so the training I received was an order of magnitude better than anything in the civilian dive schools in the states. For example, on our first open water dive, we did an emergency ascent from 95 feet. We stood on the ocean floor and waited our turn, at which point the instructor asked if we were ready to go up. After affirming, he shut off my air and I took the regulator out of my mouth and began to blow tiny bubbles, at which point he released me to go up. Since you cannot ascend faster than 60 feet per minute, from 95 feet, a minute and 35 seconds is the fastest you could surface. This means you continually exhale for that long. Ascending faster than this can cause decompression sickness, aka, "The Bends". Safety divers were stationed every 15-20 feet on the way up. After this, anytime I dove at a normal depth of 45-60 feet I never worried about an equipment malfunction since you already made it up from 95 feet without any additional air. It made me a better, more confident diver.

I would dive nearly every day that I could, spearing lapu-lapu (grouper), which was the preferred fish in the Philippines, along with some lobster. I would take these to my favorite bar and give them to the mama-san, who would cook dinner for all the working girls plus me! I was well liked, obviously, because they got to eat quite well and I got free drinks in return, plus developed friendships.

One day after we got back home to Whidbey, my friend Garrel asked me if I could change the prop on his boat underwater so he would not have the expense of pulling it out. He showed me the prop puller tool I would need to use and I said, "Yeah, I could do that under water". Well prop change was successful. As I was swimming around Garrel's boat, the owner of the next boat over asked me if I could do an inspection on his boat bottom. I suddenly got the idea for a part time job, better than pumping gas for minimum wage.

I did some research on barnacle growth and found that in this area it took approximately 6-8 weeks for a barnacle larvae to hatch. I developed a plan to do underwater maintenance on boats and clean them every 6 weeks, which would keep them growth free. I also would change props, replace zinc anodes, and even got to raise 2 boats that sunk, the largest being a 36 foot sailboat, the other a 21 foot power boat. The business grew and provided me with lots of extra party money. I would even get calls when people dropped their wallets or purses into the water at the marina. Back then I charged $25 for what I referred to as a "house call", which was to come to the marina, suit up, and retrieve the stuff that you lost.

The county sheriff did not have divers at that time so we got to help out. Once we did some rescue training for them out on the ice on Pass Lake. We made a hole in the ice and just had to hang out there in the hole in the water waiting for the volunteer firemen to practice frozen lake rescue. They put their ladders across the ice out to the hole where we floated and they pulled us out and got us back to shore.

When I got discharged and moved back to New York, I started hanging out at a local dive shop in Yonkers, Martini Dive Shop. Eventually I was asked by one of the instructors to safety dive for his classes. But of course, it was fun. I used to read the advertisements in my Skin Diver magazine, "Dive in the Philippines only $3,000 for a week". It gave me a new appreciation for what I had taken for granted when I was there in the Navy and did every day for free.

The Wrecks of the East Coast

The wreck diving in New York was also great. Of course the visibility was nothing compared to the Philippines, however you could get 50' out in the ocean on the wrecks. My favorite boat to go wreck diving on was the RV Yahoo, skippered by Steve Bielinda. It was a 55 foot fast cruiser. Steve knew how to put you right on the spots. Most of the wrecks were on the deeper side ranging from U.S.S. San Diego at 110 ft. deep, to the Andrea Doria at 240 ft. deep.

The San Diego was an armored cruiser (ACR-6), which struck a mine deployed by the German U-boat U-1536 on July 19, 1918. The ship's sinking, to the ocean floor 100 to 110 feet deep some six miles south of Long Island's Fire Island, was the only major U.S. Navy warship sunk during the war. Artifacts that could be found, if you made your way into the wreck, included lots of 30-06 ammo and the prize would be a 5 inch powder canister. This was a copper canister with oak slats on it and bronze caps, approximately 48" tall which held 2 silk bags of black powder nuggets that looked like tootsie rolls. I had a canister until we recently moved, and the wife won that argument.

Off the coast of Long Island there was also the German U boat U-853. I bet most Americans never realize we sunk a German U boat that close to our shores. It is one of the more popular dive sites in Southern New England. The hull has depth charge blast holes: one forward of the conning tower at the radio room and another in the starboard side of the engine room. Entering the wreck is dangerous due to debris, sharp metal edges, and confined spaces. At least 2 sport divers have been killed diving this wreck.

And then there is the Andrea Doria. SS Andrea Doria, was an ocean liner for the Italian Line, home-ported in Genoa, Italy, known for her sinking in 1956, where 46 people died. By Steve Bielenda's tally, 18 people have died on excursions to the Doria, known as the Mount Everest of diving because of its allure and difficulty. She is located about 50 miles southeast of Nantucket sitting in 240 feet depth where the water is just 42 degrees with very strong currents.

Several Diving Vacations

Too many to write about in detail but worth mentioning. There was the trip to Costa Rica to visit family there, with cousins Victor and Pete. While there we rented a house on the beach for 3 nights along with a young man who had an 18' boat. He took us out diving a couple of times a day. The water on the Pacific side was amazing and reminded me of the P.I. We stayed in Playa del Coco.

Playa del Coco, Costa Rica

Uncle Carl was amazed when on the drive to the shore we stopped at a Beverage center and came out with 6 cases of beer. He could not believe that we were planning to drink that much beer, 5 guys and 2 girls. The entire 3 days cost about $300 including gas, the boat rental and the kid that owned and skippered the boat, food and drink. Pretty reasonable in my opinion, so Victor, Pete and I picked up the tab for all of it.

Tortola B.V.I.

And then there was the Tropic Bird, a 110 foot live aboard dive boat ported in Tortola B.V.I. Hands down the best diving vacation I ever took. This was a 1 week trip that gave you the opportunity to make 3-4 day dives and a night dive per day, which is a lot, if you understand underwater physiology and the effects of nitrogen on your body. The high point was diving the wreck of the HMS Rhone, a 310' long UK Royal Mail Ship owned by the Royal Mail Steam Packet Company.

H.M.S. Rhone

She was wrecked off the Coast of Salt Island in the British Virgin Islands on 29 October 1867 in a hurricane, killing 123 people. Sitting in 100 feet of water with 100+ feet visibility, you can see her resting on the bottom from the surface.

The Prop **The pipe is actually the prop shaft**

I took about 150+ pictures during this week of amazing diving. Someday I will transfer them from slides to digital format.

Though I have not dived in years, I have over 4,000 hours underwater to date. Diving became my drug, the ultimate escape from reality. While 60 feet underwater, the only thing you hear is the sound of your inhaling and exhaling. Your mind is wiped clean of whatever thoughts were occupying it at the surface and it was now just you and the environment you were in. Maybe again someday.

4.

Life After the Navy

I was discharged on April 1, 1980, no joke. I had over 8 years in and if I shipped over once more for 4, then I would have had 12 years in, more than half way to retirement. At that point I would have had to commit to 20 years to get the pension. Carter was president at the time and he had nearly frozen our pay for the past 3 years, so it was an easy decision to get out. Also, in February I had found out that my mother was terminally sick with cancer, so when April 1st came I had already decided to scratch the idea of a career with Boeing and head back to N.Y. to help my mother.

The first week in April, 1980, I drove back to The Bronx and had my personal belongings shipped to my father's house in Long Island, ready to fill up his basement. This was about 2 weeks before Mt. Saint Helen erupted. As it turned out we actually got more ash in the Bronx than my friends on Whidbey Island did, which is 150 or so miles from the volcano, because of how the Jetstream moves. I moved in with my mom and my grandmother. One morning I woke up and my grandmother showed me what a great job she had done cleaning my favorite coffee mug from the Navy, which had not been washed for over 7 years. This is not gross, it is a navy tradition. It takes years to break in a new coffee mug. Well she soaked it in bleach and got it looking like new again.

My first order of business after unpacking and getting set up was to find a job. My mother took me clothing shopping for a suit to wear for job interviews. We picked out a Yves St. Laurent 3 piece wool suit beige in color. I had numerous interviews with 1 offer. The offer was from Grumman Aerospace in Bethpage Long

Island. The only problem, the job they offered me was to be a Tech Rep for their A-6, the same A-6 I worked on for all my years in the Navy. The position was for support at Whidbey Island Naval Air Station, which is exactly where I had just moved from to be back in New York! That was obviously not going to work.

So as summer approached, I went to work for my cousin Pete, who was a roofing and siding contractor. It was hard work especially in the heat of the summer, but it gave me money and experience that I would later use when I eventually built my own house. More about that to come. Cousin Victor was already working for Pete so I joined the team along with my other cousins, Pete's 2 younger brothers.

Summer was good, lots of work and lots of partying on the weekends. Vic lived down the block from me in the Bronx so we typically carpooled out to the Island where Pete lived. Unfortunately my mother's health continued to decline.

There were many days I had to take mom to a doctor or hospital for various tests. The cancer started in her colon, and after surgery, radiation and chemo we were all trying to be optimistic. But then it metastasized from her colon to her lung. She went into Albert Einstein Hospital in the Bronx, for a lobectomy where they removed the entire lobe of the effected lung. I still had WA plates on my car and the plate number started with MD so I used to get to park in the doctor's lot because they thought I was an MD (in NY doctors have MD on their plate).

Mom needed lots of extra help so she stayed at my Cousin Josie's house because her 2 daughters were nurses and could help. Eventually her case would be moved to Sloan Kettering Hospital in Manhattan, one of the Cadillac cancer facilities. Of course, when these kind of hard times come it is a blessing to have family that is willing to help. That's how it was in the old days. When someone had surgery they went to a relative's house to recover. I remember when Aunt Judy had her gallbladder out (the old fashioned way) which had a long recovery time, she stayed with us in my grandmother's room for several weeks. People actually came to visit, unlike today where you're lucky if you get a message or a like on Facebook. Nobody was sent to nursing homes, family took care of family. Assisted living was when you went to a brother, sister, niece, nephew or grandchild's place and they assisted you. Mom went back into the hospital in November never to come home again, until December 15th when she went home to the Lord.

In September I went back to college. My mother always told me I should be a lawyer, because I always had to have the last word. Well, I actually decided engineering was the route for me, taking 14 credits per semester at night and working 60 hours per week as an apprentice electrician in Local 3, IBEW in New York City. I stayed with my grandmother in the same apartment I grew up in. My aunts and uncles took care of the finances for their mother and I gave my time. In November 1982, grandma went to join mom and Uncle Luke with the Lord. At that point I moved out and got an apartment in Country Club in the Bronx, a very Italian neighborhood.

Local 3 IBEW

I continued to go to school and put in my time in the Electrical Apprenticeship which was 5 years. I got to work on a very diverse number of jobs during that time. It was mostly all commercial work including new high rise buildings in the city. I also worked at the Domino sugar plant in the Williamsburg area of Brooklyn. The most memorable part of this job was the smell. This was the plant where they processed raw sugar into white sugar and molasses. The place reeked of the smell of molasses which was quite sickening. I was only there a few months. When I finished the apprenticeship and got my Journeyman's card, the first job I got was the foreman on a residence, but not just any residence. This was a $4 million electrical contract on a 22 room duplex penthouse owned by Phil Donahue and Marlow Thomas, on 5th Avenue overlooking Central Park. The place was totally gutted and it required its own 400 amp 3 phase electrical service plus all the wiring for 22 rooms. I worked that job several months with 2 apprentices helping me. I got to meet regularly with the Donahues. Phil was a pretty nice guy, Marlo…. Well let's just say for me, NOT "That Girl".

I became a CPR instructor for the Red Cross and studied Advanced First Aid, and started conducting classes for the electrician's union. I probably certified a couple of hundred in CPR, but only had the opportunity to use it once on a friend's 2 year old, (who they later found out had some kind of medical issue), and revived him before the EMTs showed up.

One day I was working a job in the city. It was a big trench job, the whole job site was dug up as it was just being started. Well, during my morning coffee break, I was watching a laborer direct the operator of a hoe ram who was breaking out rock, when he suddenly grabbed his chest. At first I thought the guy was having a heart attack, but as I ran to him I saw the blood pumping out of his chest. A piece of steel had splintered off the ram hitting him, and severed his pulmonary artery (which I later found out from the hospital). I took charge and immediately administered first aid to hold the artery closed and minimize his blood loss. We put him on a stretcher to move him off the job area to where an ambulance could get to him. The EMS team arrived in about 5 minutes and the doctors said he would have bled out in less than 10 minutes. He underwent significant micro surgery to repair the artery. I was very touched to receive a Life Saving award and a card from his wife and children.

 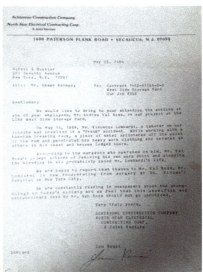

Of course, it is nice to be recognized with an award, but the best was knowing the good deed that you did, and the positive impact it had on his family. It is just one event like this that makes all the hours of training you went through well worth it. I often wonder if he is still around. I tried to locate him and his family, with no luck so far. I would have liked to send a letter and see how they all are doing, since I still have the envelope that the below card came in with the return address. Funny how when you are young you don't think about staying connected with certain people but when you get older you have a different perspective on things like that.

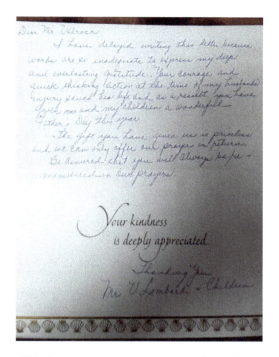

It still brings tears to my eyes reading this card

Sometimes you may wonder what God's plan was for you, and then an event like this happens and you think you got your answer for now. We will see what plans the future holds.

My life blessing of Grace

I had decided after breaking up with my last girlfriend, not to bother trying to meet someone since I was going to be moving back to Washington in a year or two. And then as John Lennon said, "Life is what happens to you while you're busy making other plans". One night in November 1984, along came Grace. We had our first date at Clams Casino in Fort Lee, New Jersey, where I told her right then and there that I had no plans to stay in New York and was moving back to Whidbey Island. She thought I was nuts saying this on our first date. After dating for a while, I got a message from God that this was the one. One evening, while hugging I looked at her face and there appeared before me the face of Jesus Christ.

I knew this was clearly a message from the Almighty that she was the one. We got engaged in February 1986 and married in January 1987.

We got married on Super bowl Sunday in New York, and New York was in the Super bowl that year. Wedding reservations at the catering hall are usually made at least a year in advance, so we had no way of knowing it was going to be Super bowl Sunday. We still had over 150 people attend, some with their portable TVs, and had the DJ announce the score from time to time. It was a great event!

My last big job in New York was as a foreman on a new 40 story high-rise in the Wall Street area. After I graduated college it was time to think about when to move back to Whidbey Island to build a house on the 2.5 acres I had bought in 1983. I made arrangements with the union to have me laid off so I could qualify for unemployment benefits when I left. We rented a 32 foot truck, packed our stuff and got out of town, towing our new Honda Prelude behind it.

We drove cross country making a few scenic stops. DO NOT ever drive up to the top of Mount Rushmore with a long rig because once you start up you cannot turn around, so you are committed. This was my 12th time driving across but a first for Grace. We stopped and visited some friends and family along the way.

When we arrived in WA, we went to our friend Donna's house to unload. She had a giant steel building, probably 50'x100' in which she allowed us to store our stuff until we finished building.

Building our first home

The first thing to do was to mark off the property lines and get out the chainsaw. The 2.5 acres was fully treed with alder, fir and hemlock. It was the first week in May, 1988 and the stinging nettles were already 3 feet tall. Even with thick work jeans on, the front of my legs were numb from the nettles by the end of the day. I found the only thing to stop them was yellow vinyl rain pants.

Once the 4 corners were found and marked I then had to lay out where the house would be, taking into account the southern exposure I needed to compliment the passive solar design. Once marked out, I started cutting in the driveway from the road.

Grace stayed with me for about 2 weeks to ensure I was starting off ok. She then flew back to New York and stayed with her parents and continued to work until I was ready for her to come back out.

Once the driveway was in, it was time to clear the building site. Every tree was cut by hand leaving the stumps about 2 ft high so I could get someone to come in with a Cat later and pop them out and do some grading.

There was enough firewood to heat the house for a few years by the time I was done. Next I built my workshop, a 14x16 building I designed, which became my temporary residence. I had a sleeping bag, Coleman stove and all the luxuries of camping. First thing every morning was to put on a pot of coffee.

My buddy Bob came over with his back hoe and we dug out for the footings and foundation, about 3 feet deep to the really hard layer. The freeze depth is only 6 inches here but I put the footings at 36 inches, which proved to be wise, because 30 years later there was not one crack in any drywall from settling.

Then the real fun started, putting in the forms for the footings. I bought 2x8s for the floor beams of the 2nd floor, and used them as the footing forms, then washed them to reuse for the floor beams. The 8"x16" footings were way over the code of 6"x12" for a single story house. So was the amount of steel I put in it.

The prep for the slab was complete.

A 12 mil vapor barrier, 4 inches of insulation with 10 inches of sand, monolithic beams carved out and steel installed, and 5" of steel reinforced concrete made for a great thermal mass that can store a lot of passive solar energy. The first week in July we poured 30 cubic yards of 4,000 PSI mix concrete, which was 3 truckloads continuous pouring. I got a few Navy guys from the base to help, gave them shovels and rakes and then all the burgers and beer they could consume when done.

I would write to Grace every week and send her pictures of the progress. We also spoke on the phone to coordinate things that she needed to be involved in. After the concrete cured for a week I started framing. First level was framed in probably a week, by me and my helper Josh, an 11 year old neighbor. He wanted $2 per hour (1988) and came over every day. Great kid and he learned a lot, including the practical use of geometry!

Me walking on top of the walls

Second story was to start next. The roof rafters for the dining room and living room were 2x12s, 32 feet long. I paid a premium for those lengths. Josh would hand me a 2x12 and I would pull it up and nail it, walking on the edges of the last 2 rafters I put into place. Today I'm lucky that I can walk on terra firma!

By September the framing was done, windows were in, roof was on and siding was up. I could now concentrate on inside wiring and plumbing.

Grace came to visit and inspect the progress. She had been staying with her parents and working up until then. I had not looked for work yet, as I needed to get the house to a point that we could move in. She came back out permanently in October and we spent our first night in our new home drinking champagne out of plastic cups.

First night

Note only the bedroom and master bath was dry walled and painted and the rest of the house was still just studs and insulation.

After that it was one room at a time, drywall, taped and painted. Since I could not find someone to do smooth wall taping I ended up doing it myself. I hate texturing and that's all they want to do, to cover up a shitty taping job.

In October I went down and applied for a job at Boeing. I wasn't sure up until now when to apply for work because what if the house wasn't weather tight yet and they wanted me to start next week? So I waited until then. In the meantime, I took a temporary job as an electrical foreman on a large housing renovation job in Navy Housing, where they were gutting all the WW2 homes and renovating including complete electrical service and wiring. I did that for a few months and made a few bucks to live off of, while working one room at a time completing drywall, taping and painting.

The first winter was a little tough as we did not have a garage door up yet and we had an unusual snow storm, 24" of snow and the temps dropped to 8 degrees for a week. I hung the blankets we used to move to close the garage door opening, and put a portable space heater in the garage to protect the plumbing.

By the following spring we were pretty much done except for flooring which was done by May, so 12 months from cutting the first tree down to completing the last of the marble and porcelain tile floors. Not bad for a one-man show with a little help from my friends!

Of course, as you homeowners know, once the house is done you now start your multiyear job of landscaping and all the other little things that never end. We have many memories in this home that we built, parties, BBQs, company and political events to mention a few.

The first few years Grace's parents would come out and stay the summer. It was great to have them as they were always good company. Elena was an awesome cook and Carmine was a hard worker always looking for me to give him projects to do while I was at work. They helped get our perennial flower garden planted in their first summer out. Carmine was also an awesome first mate when we went out fishing on my boat. I'll never forget once when we came home from fishing for salmon with a bucket of fresh herring I planned to use for bait the next time fishing. Well by the time I got out of the shower the herring were all breaded and fried! Elena was so proud of the dinner she cooked for us, it broke my heart to tell her that was supposed to be bait for tomorrow's salmon fishing trip.

We had sit down dinners for up to 20 friends in our first home. BBQs of up to 100 people for political events with Congressmen and State Legislators in attendance, as well as a sit down fundraiser dinner for Attorney General Rob McKenna.

We did some of the family traditional dinners in our home over the years with friends that became our new family. Typically we would entertain for Thanksgiving and Christmas Eve. Christmas Eve was the traditional Feast of Seven Fishes, all seafood. This tradition continues even today, though some of our friends have moved but some new ones have been added to the invite list.

In November of 2004, we had a family reunion cruise of the Benedetto family. Cousin Anita and Chuck decided they would get married on that cruise, though they kept it a secret. They figured so many of the family, 93 of us, were there already. They made arrangements for the Night Club for their private reception in the afternoon when it's normally closed to the general public.

Here is a group shot of us. A great reunion and time to do it again!

I thought I was going to retire and die of old age in this house, but then my knees decided differently. The steps started getting more difficult so we talked about the "retirement home" with no steps. In June 2017, just before retiring, we found a great .55 acre water view lot to build on just 2 miles from our current house. The seller was very motivated so we did well with negotiating price. I knew it would be sad to sell it someday.

    The view from our lot   1000' private community beach

We found the house we wanted at a home show, 1 level, with a great 1300 sq. ft. garage. I got the builder to agree to let me do much of the finish work to cut the price. We started clearing in June 2019. I did all the interior painting, flooring, and the flat concrete work in the garage and out front with help from friends. In the preceding months, we had bought appliances, lighting and plumbing fixtures during all the major sales, typically got 40% - 50% off. All in all this saved us enough money, which made the difference of affording the place or not.

Because we did not want a daylight basement or any steps, we had to do major excavating to bring the uphill side of the lot down 9 feet and move all the dirt to the low side of the lot.

The result was no steps and no railing on the deck to obstruct the view, but lots of retaining walls to terrace it off. A total of 1,440 blocks (6' x 17", 66 lbs. each) were put in once again, with help from a few friends. I am so done with blocks, LOL.

We moved into the new place the last week in February 2020, and had our first guest, Grace's sister Nancy, stay with us for a bit. She helped us pack and clean the last of the stuff from the old house. We listed the old house for sale but then along came the Communist Chinese Virus which pretty much shut down the real estate business. However, we did finally sell it the first week in August 2020. That was a big relief! We spent the summer doing landscaping, planting shrubs and building block walls (yuk). At least all those projects kept me busy during the CCV lockdown, so I had plenty of things to keep me from getting bored, because those that know me know I cannot just sit around. And if I ever think I am out of projects, there is always the never-ending Honey Do list! The last semi-major project will be to pour 140 feet of concrete on the driveway sometime this summer. While we were building, I put in electrical provisions for radiant heat on the bottom 50 feet of the driveway, to keep the ice melted and a place to stop before reaching the road.

Next year we will have new neighbors on the last vacant lot near us. A year ago, our close friends Bill and Renee bought the lot across the street from us so we won't have to get into the car and drive to visit them in the future.

5.

A Career at Boeing

When we started to build our first home, it was difficult to decide when to start looking for work. We had saved enough money to buy the materials to build and get the house complete less floors and finish items. It was important to not use this money for food or living. The timing for a job became a quandary because you never know how long after you apply you may get called to start, so I ended up not applying until October '88, after the house was weather tight and the master bedroom and bath were finished, except floors.

   I applied for an engineering position and got a letter from Boeing saying how interested they were in me and that I was in their "skill file". No phone number to follow up or any other info was provided. Well I waited a month and then went down and looked at the openings posted, and saw a position for a flight line avionics technician, an hourly job. I applied for that since it was what I did in the Navy, and at this point I wanted to get my foot in the door. I got called, interviewed and started the end of February. My boss ended up being a former boss of mine when I was in the Navy, Mike Eisner, great guy.

   My first objective was to find a phone book and make a connection in engineering so I could transfer. As a flight line technician, I worked daily with Liaison Engineering so the connection was made and I transferred to a Salary exempt position in engineering after a couple of months. I worked in Liaison engineering for about a year, which was actually very good experience for my later years at Boeing because there was a lot of hands on experience on the planes, as opposed to what I called Armchair engineers that sat at their desk.

When the machinist union went on strike there was not much work to do on the flight line, so I got loaned out for a few months to a design project engineering group. I loved it and they loved me. The chief engineer told me that as soon as I go back to Liaison after the strike is over, apply for a transfer, which I did. I spent my remaining 25+ years in Cabin Systems Design engineering group. After a couple of years I became a Lead engineer in a group responsible for the inflight entertainment systems (IFE) on the planes, where I worked for over 20 years.

Business Travel

I had the opportunity to travel on business in this position. There were many monthly trips to Orange County, CA, where several of the major IFE equipment suppliers were as well as a couple of test facilities. All new equipment required Electromagnetic Interference testing and Environmental testing which we typically witnessed/observed. Every new piece of equipment has to go through rigorous testing to ensure it does not emit any electromagnetic energy that can interfere with other aircraft systems. Also we had to test to ensure it would not be susceptible to normal aircraft electrical environment as well as thermal, vibration, shock, humidity and other conditions. The testing was fun and challenging, especially when it failed to show compliance. Although it was the supplier's responsibility to show compliance to all of these various requirements, we did assist them in redesign and offer suggestions. Even though a unit may pass all the required lab testing, the final test was to flight test it on the airplane. So another facet of this job that I loved was test flights to certify new equipment and demonstrate before the FAA that the equipment performed its intended function and did not interfere with other systems.

Japan

Two of our suppliers, Panasonic and Jamco, were in Japan. I got to make trips to Japan about twice a year for various meetings and testing.   Panasonic was located in Osaka Japan, which was mostly an industrial area. **Jamco was located in** Tachikawa, a city located in the western portion of Tokyo Metropolis.

The suppliers were always very courteous hosts when we visited. Panasonic had an annual meeting that I called a "SushiFest", since it was attended by mostly managers, and seemed like a big "dog and pony show" with major effort in entertaining them. Interesting, we always hear about how hard the Japanese work, as though Americans don't, but anytime I was there it was always them that would say, "That's enough, time to go home and come back tomorrow". I'm not saying they were not hard workers, what I am saying is we work at least as hard.

Jamco once developed a new video entertainment projector. The testing was to be at a lab in Nara Japan. This was an all day trip from my hotel in Tokyo. First we took a regular train to the bullet train, then the bullet train to Kyoto station where we took a small private train to the lab facility in Nara. It was a fun trip as there were no Americans in sight, so I got to really experience the Japanese businessman's life. We stayed in a Japanese businessman's hotel in Nara, and my hosts from Jamco kept apologizing for the accommodations not being like a western hotel. It kind of reminded me of a cabin on a cruise ship. You even had to step up over the threshold to get into the bathroom, which was obviously a modular bathroom installed in the hotel room. After work we had drinks at a local tavern that also served various things to eat at the bar, all prepared by the bartender. My host kept ordering some very strange things for me to try. In

Japanese culture, "saving face" is important, so no matter what they gave me to eat, I would smile and say "Oishi", which means delicious. Well this only brought on the next order of something even more strange, but no matter I would not surrender, I had to "save face". Every plate got worse than the one before it, and they finally gave up and said to me "you are a very strange American". They also made the same mistake as the Chinese hosts in Beijing, thinking they could drink an American Navy veteran under the table. These 2 guys were half my body weight. You can figure the rest out yourself.

Once at the lab, I was on top of a vibration test unit looking something over when I felt severe shaking of the test unit. I thought somebody turned the vibration unit on. Then I looked up and noticed everybody was shaking and realized we were having an earthquake! It was ironic this happened when I was on the vibration test unit.

Seoul

I also made trips to support airlines in various capacities. My first international trip for work was in support of Asiana Airline's delivery of their first 747-400, in Seoul. These "Meet and Greet" trips were typically 6 weeks long with a small group of key engineers and instructor pilots. For the Boeing engineers, the mission was to keep the plane flying and to teach the airline engineers how to keep the plane flying. A plane sitting on the ground does not generate any revenue.

I stayed in the most awesome hotel called the Shilla Hotel. Anyone that was anyone stayed at the Shilla when in Seoul. One night when I returned from work, I noticed a line of black SUVs with guys that had wires coming out of their ears. They looked like U.S. Feds. As I walked through the revolving door into the lobby, there stood Secretary of Defense Dick Cheney and General

Colin Powell just 10 feet in front of me. I slowly approached them and put out my hand to shake and greeted them. I later found out that President HW Bush was going to be staying there too, but that would be after I left. The hotel had the most phenomenal spa facility that made the New York Health and Racquet Club look like a YMCA.

My work hours were dictated by the flight schedule of the plane we delivered, and, since I didn't have to be at work till 3pm every day, I spent many hours at the spa during the day. And for $20 you could get a massage in your room for an hour! Interesting, I noticed the massage therapists were blind. I guess it is good that a blind person can still have some sort of career. I did not know this at first, but when she entered the room I could see that look on her face. She nonchalantly touched me and felt my robe, and she said to get undressed. Since every country has different protocols regarding how undressed you should get for massage, I asked her "no underwear"? She replied, "it does not matter I cannot see". She was awesome and I wanted the same girl again so I asked her name. She said….. Number 5. So I would call and make a reservation for Number 5.

Since this was my first long trip I decided to bring Grace there for week 3 and 4, so she flew to Seoul and met me. We spent Thanksgiving there, invited to the resident Boeing rep's house for a traditional Thanksgiving dinner. We got to tour some old Palaces and do lots of shopping in Itaewon. Itaewon is known for its cosmopolitan dining and nightlife, with Korean BBQ restaurants, and upscale bistros, as well as low-key kebab shops catering to a late-night crowd. Casual beer bars and gay pubs sit alongside hip dance clubs. And you can shop till you drop! Grace also liked Number 5 a few times while she was there with me, though she almost threw her off her back. Once again it was my fault (I'm the husband) because I called the room and she jumped when the phone rang as Number 5 was walking on her back.

Uzbekistan

This was a very interesting trip. This was in support of a 1 day sales meeting with Uzbekistan Airlines buying some 767s. It took 2 days to get there and 2 days to get home. At that time there were no hotels in Tashkent that Boeing approved us to stay in, so we were put up in some former Soviet military officer's quarters. It was like a small apartment building. I was told bring your own food and bring your own water! So my 1 carry-on bag had a change of clothes, 2 - 2 liter bottles of water, canned tuna, dried fruit, jerky and 2 rolls of toilet paper. As I later learned I would have been better off just bringing my backpack with all my camping equipment because my room had no heat and it was freaking cold. It did have a refrigerator so I backed it up to my bed and left the door open so it would run all night throwing off heat from the coils. The toilet paper they provided was like the cardboard on the back of a pad of paper, maybe good for scraping but not for wiping. The housekeeping people were very friendly. The first morning I woke up quite jet lagged and went down at around 0430 in search of coffee. They were sitting drinking tea and invited me to join them. There were 4 of them, sharing a piece of bread the size of my fist with a jar of jam no more than 1 ounce. They offered some of it to me. How generous, but sad, so I told them using body language that I was so full, but thank you. We had lots of conversations, though they spoke no English and I only knew 4 words in Russian. It was all by sign & body language. When I departed they were very happy that I gifted them with all my leftover food and toilet paper.

The Philippines

About 10 months after Mount Pinatubo erupted, which was in June of 1991, I went on a sales support trip to Manila. It had been 15 years since I was last in P.I. When I left the airport to head to the hotel, I could not believe the Tagalog words that came out of my mouth, like they were never forgotten. The meetings went well and fell over a weekend that we were off. On Friday when we were finished working, I jumped on a Victory Liner bus down to Olongapo, where I spent so much time while in the Navy. When I stepped off the bus in Olongapo, I had the weirdest feeling come over me. I did not feel like I was returning after 15 years. It felt like I was returning home after a short vacation away. My friend Barry (RIP another Agent Orange victim) and his wife Ivy met me as I stepped off the bus. I served with Barry for several years in the early 70s, and spent much time with him in P.I. The Navy base was in the process of shutting down and there were very few sailors left. Town was on the quiet side and there were many sad faces on the locals. There was so much destruction from the eruption, and they knew their economy was being devastated by the communist influenced faction of the government that wanted the U.S. Navy out.

I went to Sonny's, the old hang out on Gordon Street, and had beers that night and reminisced with Barry and his wife Ivy, who was still stationed there as part of the last of the group shutting the base down. At the old hang out bar, Mamasan asked me how I was going to get back to Manila. I told her I would take the Victory Liner. She was surprised and told me it was dangerous now and introduced me to a young 17 year old girl that just started working at the bar. She directed the girl to escort me back to Manila and ensure my safety, stay the night, and don't take any money from me. I laughed and thanked her and told her that would not be necessary. I stayed at Barry's house that night in base housing. We drove through the base to see the remains of the enlisted Sky Club in Cubi Point that had collapsed from the weight of all the volcanic ash after it rained, as did many of the other buildings in the area. On Sunday afternoon I took the bus back to Manila, alone, for our last day of meetings on Monday morning.

China

I got to make several trips to China, twice to Beijing and once to Xiamen.

Xiamen

Xiamen was a sales support trip for 2 days. I had a great connection for getting a visa. Instead of mailing my passport to the Chinese Consulate in CA, there was a guy in Hong Kong we used since no visa was required to enter Hong Kong. I would fax him a day ahead with my arrival and hotel info. He would meet me at the hotel, the Shangri La, which was a very nice place in the Kowloon side of Hong Kong. I would give him my passport and pictures and he would then meet me back at the hotel in the morning with the passport and visa. So easy plus it gave me an excuse to overnight in Hong Kong which has great shopping and night life.

In Xiamen, we were put up in some kind of apartment type housing. At 2am, someone knocked at, opened the door and came into my room. It was the manager along with some military guy with guns. They were checking to see if you had a hooker in your room! The next morning I asked the resident Boeing rep what would happen if you did. It's a shake down for money, you give them $500 and the problem goes away. That is one reason why when I always traveled internationally with a few thousand dollars in U.S. Ben Franklins… you never know.

When I got to the airport to return home, I went to the Xiamen Airlines counter to check in. I was told my reservation was cancelled. I asked why and they told me I did not reconfirm 72 hours before departure. I told them I hadn't even arrived 72 hours before departure! The plane was still there at the gate. I said "can't I get on that plane?". She said no, that they had rules. They knew who I was so I had to be careful because I didn't want my reaction to have an effect on the sale of the planes to them. They told me it was no problem (ya for them maybe) and that I would be booked on the next flight to Hong Kong in several hours. They told me I had to buy a new ticket, which was NOT sold at that counter, so they gave me a driver to go to another place to get a ticket. Well they did not take American Express, which is what Boeing used as a corporate card at that time, so once again it's a good thing I had a pocket full of Ben Franklins. Since they did not take U.S. currency, I had to get the driver to take me to the money exchange to change them to Yuan. What a cluster F***! I had to call the Shangra La hotel in Hong Kong and book an overnight since I was now going to miss my connecting flight from Hong Kong to Seattle. Eventually I was on the plane, in first class, and the guy sitting behind me got on the plane and was furious, exclaiming how they cancelled his reservation! I said to him, "didn't you reconfirm 72 hours before departure?". I had to tell him the same thing happened to me because he was not happy.

There were 2 trips to Beijing, one for sales support and one for fixing a 737 with some EMI (Electromagnetic Interference) problems. The latter was for a week so of course it was more eventful. The plane was being used to fly some Chinese Airforce General around so it was located on a Military installation. A representative from the Civil Aviation Administration of China, (CAAC) was supposed to meet us at the gate to escort us in. Well

I guess someone forgot to tell the gate guard because when we arrived he shoved is SKS rifle in our faces and screamed at us in Chinese. We were scared to death because we had no idea WTF he was saying. Thank God the CAAC guy showed up just a minute or two later before any shots were fired, and got it straight.

When we went to the plane we noticed a Chinese soldier with a machine gun at each plane on the flight line. I advised my work colleagues that if they had to go pee, they shouldn't wait until the last minute and run. Walk nice and slowly. The entertainment audio was interfering with the VHF Communication radio in the flight deck. We were not able to confirm it for more than a day because there was some local noise that was a much higher level than the emissions from the entertainment system. We suspected they had jammers going on the base. Every time we approached them to shut the jammers down they denied their existence. So we made a simple direction finder and connected it to our spectrum analyzer. The CAAC guy was amazed at our intelligence when we slowly turned until we got the strongest signal, then pointed and said, "there it is, shut it down or we're going home". So they agreed to shut it down for 15 minutes each hour. Needless to say this made a 1 day troubleshooting job take 5 days.

They were very gracious host in spite of the experiences with the guards. They took us on a tour of the Great Wall

Tiananmen Square - for those of you that remember the massacre here - troops armed with assault rifles and accompanied by tanks fired at the demonstrators and those trying to block the military's advance into Tiananmen Square

They fed us lunch every day and at the end when we fixed the plane they threw a big party for us 6 Boeing engineers and a dozen or so military and government people. The Chinese show the importance or regard for their guests by how many dishes they serve. We were served about 25 dishes. There were some very interesting things served. For example, a dish of turtles (headless), and then later a dish of turtle soup with the heads. I learned to be a very rich delicacy reserved for only the most important guests, was frog ovary soup. I want to know WHO thinks of this stuff! They also served some horrible tasting liquor and thought they were going to drink us under the table forcing us to do shots with them. Little did they know... until they had to carry out half of their Army Officers.

Bombay

My trip to Bombay was twofold. First, it was discovered that a wire bundle was missing from the 747-400 delivered to Air India. I was part of the AOG (Airplane On the Ground) team to do the repair. After which, I was to stay behind for 6 weeks to train their engineers as this was their first 747-400 delivered.

Every day when the plane returned we finished off all the leftovers from First Class

Everyone was very friendly and nice. We had good times training the flight crews and engineers on how to maintain and operate the aircraft.

Bombay was the filthiest place I had ever seen in all the countries I had ever visited. It seemed one third of its population lived under blue tarps on the street. As I walked to work one morning I saw poop all over the place in this one area. I figured this must be a popular place to walk your dog, until the next day I walked there just before sun up and saw all the people, no dogs. It was the only place I had ever been where I saw people with leprosy walking around with nubs for hands, etc. And there was zero empathy from the locals because they believed these people are "supposed to be that way" because of their caste system. If you were born poor that's how it was supposed to be.

Living in the street. The apartments in the back are where a mid-income person would live

I was lucky that before I left for India, the owner of the Jack in the Box near my office was from India. I mentioned to him that I was heading there and he asked if I would bring some gifts to his parents. I said sure, and he gave me a box of stuff. When I arrived at the hotel Oberoi, his parents and brother Mario met me. I gave them the box and they invited me to have dinner at their home. Mario picked me up the next afternoon after work.

They prepared a feast and the food was awesome. As it turned out, Mario had just gotten laid off from his job so I asked him if he wanted to be my driver since he had a car. The hotel wanted 1,400 Rupees a day for a car and driver. He said he would do it for 500. I told him I would pay him 700. So Mario came every morning to pick me up and drive me to work at the airport. He lived just a mile from the airport so that was convenient for him. When I was getting ready to get off, I would call him and he would come pick me up. We would go out for dinner and drinks on the way back to the hotel, my treat. This was so awesome, having my own personal driver who became friends to hang out with and show me around.

We visited lots of different and sometimes strange places. There was a park that had caves carved by hand hundreds of years ago by Buddhist monks.

There was no happy ending to this trip as I came home with malaria, but all part of the memories that make up a life of blessings.

Italy

This was a great trip and how it came to be is kind of funny. Grace was going to New York for a 50th Anniversary of her Uncle and Aunt, and a family wedding, with several weeks in between. Her sister and husband were going to go to Italy for 2 family weddings there in between the New York events. I told her to go to N.Y. for the occasions and fly to Italy in between. Well one day I asked my boss, "Do we have anything going on in Italy?" He replied, "we have a nightmare! There are 4 Air India 777s on the flight line that we cannot deliver because there are no seats in them, because the seat supplier hasn't tested them". I asked, "Is Avio the seat supplier", and he said yes. Well Avio is in Latina, about 12 Km from where Grace was staying with the family in Sabaudia. So I told him I would go help if he needed it. He was so happy I had to confess and tell him that Grace was there. I flew to Rome for 2 weeks and stayed at the Hilton near the airport for a few days then at a hotel on the beach in Sabaudia. I rented a car and drove to work every day.

The Hilton ended up giving us a private tour of the Vatican because they screwed up and did not wake me up for work. The manager asked me how my day went and I told him how embarrassed I was to be several hours late for work, and that I would look for another hotel to stay at. So he upgraded my room to a phenomenal suite and arranged for the tour.

The seat supplier was supposed to write test procedures for us to review and approve, but had not submitted anything so my mission was to write the procedures, do the testing and write the reports. I was on the FAA's approved list for this test witnessing. Well when I got to work I immediately saw what the problem was. The Boeing procurement agent had a real attitude and when the Avio managers came into the office she started yelling at them in front of everyone. Well the one Italian guy said to the other, "Tell her to go F*** herself", in Italian. I laughed and after went to his office, introduced myself in Italian, apologized and asked for his help in writing the test procedures his company was supposed to submit. I returned to my office and 10 minutes later he came in with a stack of papers, all the test procedures they had already written but never submitted because of how they were being treated. I thanked him and went to my boss and told him the procedures were done. He didn't understand how I could have written hundreds of pages that fast. I explained to him all you had to do was ask the right way instead of yelling at them. So we went to the lab for 2 weeks of testing and all was well.

Grace got to stay with me at the hotel on the beach, which made her happy because it was over 100 degrees and the family would not turn on the air conditioning. They said they only use it when it's "hot" because it's not healthy. I told them it's over 100 degrees and the reason they don't turn it on is because they are cheap. Anyway, we had a good time and it was a successful business trip. I got home on a Sunday and my phone rang. It was my boss. He asked what I was doing next week. I told him I was going to go to a friend's wedding in CA. He told me to get my ass on a plane and get back to Rome. So I called Grace and told her I was coming back for another week. It was awesome!

California

My last 15 years at Boeing found me going to California every month for a week, mostly to Orange County, spending up to 100 nights a year there. I really enjoyed the monthly getaways and the weather was almost always very nice there, but for some reason that I could never pinpoint, I wouldn't want to live there. I stayed at the Embassy Suites in Irvine for a number of years until they pissed me off. My very good friend Dr. Cyndee told me I should stay in Huntington Beach near her, at the Hilton Waterfront.

She gave me a tour of the town and I was sold. The hotel was located on Pacific Coast Hwy., a block away from the Huntington Beach pier, right in the center of Surf City U.S.A. The hotel staff was phenomenal and I remain friends with 3 of them to this day.

One year on my birthday, I had the "do not disturb" sign on the door as I was taking a shower. The bell rang, and I thought, can't they read? I opened the door and there is the staff with a cart holding a birthday cake, a bottle of wine and a card they had all signed.

I was very touched. I felt a special kind of friendship with 2 of them that worked night shift. On a few occasions I had a PTSD attack in the hotel at night and they were there for me when I appeared in the lobby, knowing there was something wrong just by taking one look at me. Yes, Annica and Courtney, I am talking about you two awesome ladies.

They always upgraded me to an executive suite. Such personal service!

Main Street was quaint with a number of eating and drinking establishments. Breakfast was at the Sugar Shack, where I eventually was accepted by some of the locals and got to sit with them every morning. A 4 egg white omelet with spinach, avocado and cheese was one of my favorites, otherwise oatmeal with all kinds of cut up fresh fruit in it.

I discovered what eventually became my favorite steak house. The Winery restaurant in Irvine was started by 4 guys that were working at Morton's and left to open their own place. The Winery blows Morton's and Ruth Chris away. It became a regular place for me and I became friendly with the owners. They treat their customers extremely well and the food and service is beyond excellent. And as an added bonus, I met Steve there one night on the cigar patio.

c. 2014

Steve, Marina and me after an awesome steak dinner at The Winery

I kept in touch with him and every month when I went down we hung out together. He got married to an awesome lady, Marina. We have spent many hours together and shared so much.

And then there was Kelly's Cigar shop. One day I was driving around looking for Costco in Tustin. I stopped at a gas station to ask directions but nobody spoke English. I drove and stopped at a corner and asked "where is Costco"? No one spoke English. Then I saw Kelly's cigar shop and said to myself, I bet he speaks English and can tell me where Costco is. Anyway, John the owner, gave me directions and then I came back to hang out after my shopping. He had a small shop and a patio in the back where the guys and girls would have a smoke and a drink and engage in good talk.

Out on the Patio

It always made for a great social event and a place to meet and mingle. John and I became good friends, and his sister Mary had a beauty salon next door so I would get my hair cut while I was down there.

I also became friends with several of the Alaska Airlines crew, since it was common to fly with one of two or three crews whenever I flew down to Orange County each month. I am still friends with Dale Luther, who no longer is a flight attendant, and also Eric and Lilly Marks, who are both flight attendants for Alaska. Even after 20+ years Eric remembers to send me a text message every Christmas and other occasions. Recently he and his wife have become my lifesavers when I need someone to talk and pray with on those bad nights when the evil one comes out to haunt me. A 2+ hour phone call is not uncommon. Interesting how God puts people in your life and you may not realize why till many years later.

Though not connected to but was during my career at Boeing, from May 2-5 2013, over 83,000 NRA members gathered in Houston, TX to celebrate their 2nd Amendment freedom. A surprise Keynote speaker appeared on the stage and had 83,000 people in tears as she told her story. Her name was Taya Kyle, widow of the famous Navy SEAL Chris Kyle, who had just been murdered exactly 3 months prior on February 2nd. Later that evening I was gifted a ticket to the "Cigar and Brandy" event, which normally sold for thousands of dollars per ticket. While sitting there alone, Taya Kyle quietly walked onto the balcony where the event was being held. She started to walk toward my table and as she was right beside me, I stood up, embraced her, and whispered condolences in her ear. I was shocked when she then asked if she could sit and have a drink. OMG this turned out to be the highlight of the 3 days. A waitress came by with a tray of cigars and Taya and I both lit one up and sat for an hour, talking and sipping a few drinks. We talked about Chris a bit and I shared some stories about my experience diving with some Team 3 members in the P.I. when I was in the Navy. It was absolutely amazing. She told me about the upcoming movie which was later released in 2015, "American Sniper", directed by Clint Eastwood. I will never forget this blessing.

When the 787 Dreamliner program kicked off, I picked up additional responsibilities on the development of that new model airplane. I had 2 desks and shared my time between the 787 and the other existing models as Lead engineer for 2 different groups of engineers. In 2014, after my 2nd trip to the ER in 2 weeks, I took a medical leave of absence for 3 months. Working 60+

hours a week to meet the new 787 Dreamliner schedule on top of all the work we had on 777 and 747 became a bit much. In addition to work, I also sat on the Executive Board of the Washington State Republican Party and put in 30+ hours a week as a volunteer. A few days before I was to start my leave, I came down with shingles, which can be triggered by stress, so I ended up starting it earlier.

After 3 months of relaxing, including a trip to Italy to visit family, I returned to work and was asked to Lead a group of engineers in the Telecoms group, which was responsible for the Wi-Fi on the planes. It was a good job and I had a good boss who I knew for years before he became a boss. I was treated well and was well respected by my peers and management. When I started thinking about retirement, it was a difficult decision to make. If I didn't like my job it would have been easier to decide.

Three years later, I made the decision that the time had come. I had been working for 50 years and it was now someone else's time to take the reins. My last day at work was an absolute horror. In fact I didn't even get to say good bye to most of my colleagues. The night before I had a bad attack and drove to the office at 2am. I packed my desk and by 6am I was a disaster. I could not drive home with all the meds I took, so one of my engineers, Diego, and friend, Bret, drove me home in my car while the other followed. My counselor later told me that retirement can be just a stressful as getting divorced. It was a total upset to my otherwise structured life. Don't get me wrong, I'm glad I retired, but it was a difficult last night.

6.

My Other Life

No this was not some kind of secret life. This was my passion for conservative politics. In 1998, I became active in politics. When people asked me what drove me to get involved, I said, "Bill Clinton". They said, "but he is a democrat".... I said, "Exactly". My introduction was like a baptism by fire. I started by being Linda Smith's campaign chairman for her U.S. Senate race. I was also appointed to be a Precinct Chairman in our county Republican Party to fill a vacancy in my precinct.

As time went on in the next election cycle in 2000, I was asked to chair John Koster's race for the U.S. House of Representatives. At the same time I was elected to be State Committeeman. Every county had a State Committeeman and Committeewoman who represent their county and makes up the State Committee. I really enjoyed this aspect of my involvement at this higher level. It got me involved with writing the State Party platform and many other things that had a very definite impact on State level politics. John, unfortunately, did not win his race, but it did give me an opportunity to make some life friends. At one of the fundraisers we put together, we invited then Congressman Lindsey Graham, House Impeachment Manager for Clinton's impeachment, and Steve Largent, former Seattle Seahawks H.O.F., then Congressman from Oklahoma. It was a great event where I was gifted an autographed copy of the Articles of Impeachment against Bill Clinton signed by Lindsey Graham.

I also received a football inscribed to me and signed by Steve Largent.

I originally was supporting Steve Forbes for President in 2000. I did get to meet with him several times and liked the idea of an outsider running.

Then after Steve dropped out of the race, I was contacted by the GW Bush campaign asking me to assume the same leadership position I had for Forbes, for Bush. I agreed and this opened so many new doors for me. I did get to meet both Bush and Cheney on several occasions. It was very awesome whether you liked the guy or not.

    I was elected to serve at the 2000 National Convention of the Republican Party of the United States, which convened at the First Union Center in Philadelphia, Pennsylvania, from July 31 to August 3, 2000. Of the 2,000 delegates at the Washington State

Convention, only a handful get elected to go the National Convention as a Delegate or Alternate Delegate, so it is quite an honor to attend and represent your state. The delegates all pay their own way which could cost a couple of thousand dollars between the hotel, airfare and other expenses, but well worth the experience if you are lucky enough to be elected.

The convention lasts several days with many events to attend in the daytime, as the actual convention meetings are in the evening.

At one pro-life lunch event I sat with Ambassador Allen Keys, who was the keynote speaker.

Only the delegates and media are allowed on the convention floor. I bumped into Chuck Norris, and dignitaries on the floor. I was even interviewed by German media and appeared on TV. At the end of the convention, they did a huge balloon drop of red, white and blue balloons. There were so many balloons dropped that when they got over knee high the secret service had to stop the drop because nobody would be able to move around in case of emergency.

How exciting!

I was able to meet Bush the first time when he came to Boeing to speak to us. They set him up in the hanger with a 747 in the backdrop. I was at the front of the line so I got to say hello, shake hands and get an autograph from him. I also helped put together events in the area for both Bush and Cheney.

I got a call from Austin 2 days before election day to find a place within 30 minutes that can hold 5,000 people because they wanted to bring Cheney in. Well I did and I got to escort him off the plane and into the event!

We put together an event for GW Bush in Everett on the pier with the U.S.S. Abraham Lincoln in the background. Secret Service had me man the platform just beside the podium where Bush was speaking.

At the end of the event I got to speak with Bush and have him and Laura sign my Bush hat. At a later date I had Cheney and Lynne sign it also.

The platform was reserved for Veterans, I was guarding it.

Politics was rapidly becoming my new passion. Like any true passion, it drives you and gives you new found energy. After GW Bush won the election, I got an invitation to the Inaugural Ball. Of course, we immediately made airline reservations to D.C. and I called my cousin Nancy who lived in D.C. to arrange accommodations at her place. She was very gracious, but then again, that's how Italian families are! This certainly helped make the trip more affordable plus it was much more fun to stay with family than a hotel somewhere. From her house it was an easy train ride just a few stops to the Capital and the location of the Ball. We also got to visit our nephew Eric who was attending college at American University while we were in town.

How exciting to attend the Inaugural Ball! But to be honest I would not do it again. The outdoor events were freezing cold in January in D.C.

It hailed and rained and was so cold at the swearing in ceremony and the parade, but it was very exciting. Nancy knew lots of insider tips about the event, having worked on The Hill and been to several of these events.

Since Boeing was a major donor to the campaign, I contacted the Boeing Government Relations office and told them I was coming to the Ball. They put together an awesome package of gifts and tickets to various events. One event, Grace and I were the only 2 from the state of Washington to attend, Dick Cheney's Salute to American Veterans. Gerald McRaney was the M.C. and Connie Stevens sang God Bless America. One of the keynote speakers was a Jewish man, who told an amazing story about his years spent and how he survived at Auschwitz in WWII.

Dick Cheney's Salute to American Veterans

Tickets to this event was for VERY high donors, which Boeing was one. In attendance were approximately 103 of the living 108 Medal of Honor winners (I don't remember the exact count). It was very humbling to be in their presence. Dick Cheney presented a tiny lapel corsage to all that attended, made up with a red white and blue rose, which I still have today and proudly wear to appropriate events.

That night at the Ball, we ran into Jacqueline Smith and Ricky Schroeder. I'm sure there were many more but it was standing only and a lot of people. Of course everyone waited for the President and First Lady to come in and dance, followed by the Vice President and his wife.

In December 2002, I was elected to be the Chairman of the Island County Republican Party. This new position brought with it a ton of responsibility, especially if you were going to be an effective Chairman. The party was in need of some major overhaul. I was successful at getting the dead wood Precinct Committee Officers to resign and then appoint new people into those positions that were prepared to do the work required. We grew the party from a hand full of members to many, with dues receipts increasing from a few hundred dollars a year to thousands of dollars, and over 230 donors. We opened a 1,000 square foot office that we rented with half the rent donated back by the landlord. This storefront office, staffed by volunteers, gave us the visibility we needed and by the next midterm election, we had volunteers coming out of the woodwork!

2004 was an incredible election year for us. Bush was running for re-election and Rob McKenna ran for State Attorney General, plus local senate and state representative positions.

Senator Dino Rossi, me, Grace and Congressman George Nethercutt at our Lincoln Day Dinner

I chaired Rob's campaign and became friends with Rob from then forward. Rob won and I then sat on his State Advisory Council. The sad result of our Governor's race being stolen resulted in Dino Rossi loosing. Sitting on the Executive Board of the Washington State Republican Party at that time, I was intimately involved with not only the recount but also the fiduciary responsibility and met with the attorneys daily. The race gained national attention for its legal twists and extremely close finish, among the closest political races in United States election history. Dino Rossi was declared the winner in the initial automated count and again in a subsequent automated recount. But after a second recount done by hand, which was paid for by John Kerry, Democrat Christine Gregoire took the lead by a margin of 129 votes. After all the counties counted and reported their votes, except King county which was last, they suddenly found a box of ballots. They shopped this to a liberal district court judge who decided the new box of ballots would be counted. Now that a precedence had been set, an additional 10 boxes of ballots were found in King County and the race was stolen.

Also in 2004, I received the most awesome letter from President Bush.

President Bush sent me a hand written letter of thanks. What an incredible feeling!

In 2006, Vice President Cheney came to Washington. I helped out with the event and thought I was just going to attend the luncheon. Well the day before the event I got a call. I was told I was invited to the Round Table meeting, 1 hour prior to the luncheon. This Round Table was $10,000 per ticket, and I was invited as a guest. WOW! There were 6 paid ticket holders, the State Party Chair and me. Cheney walked in, we all stood and shook hands and then he said "Sit down and tell me what is on your mind". We went around the table and had about 10 minutes each with him. It was so awesome and the really amazing part was about 2 weeks later he was on the Rush Limbaugh show. I got a call from my boss telling me they were talking about me so I tuned in just as Cheney was saying that "a friend of mine that he met with a couple of weeks ago was telling me about the concern of the porosity of the northern border with Canada". He actually listened and paid attention to what I had talked to him about!

To Andrew
With Best Wishes,

My third meeting with VP Dick Cheney

September 2006, unfortunately was not a good month for me. On September 10th, as I was driving to the airport to fly to Orange

County CA for work, I got a phone call from a friend. He called to tell me that our friend Stewart had committed suicide the night before. This was a terrible shock. After landing I decided I needed to relax so I went to Kelly's for a cigar and a drink. Sitting out on the patio, unfortunately, was not relaxing because he had the big screen going with all September 11th documentaries. I had to leave. Well that evening at the hotel, I had a really bad attack and made my way to the ER. It's extra scary to go to the ER alone 1,000 miles from where you live. The ER confirmed I was not having any cardio issues but wanted to keep me overnight. So I went up to a room but by 9am I had not seen another doctor yet and I was calming down so I signed myself out, called Alaska Airlines and changed my flight home. I saw my doctor and they did a stress test which I passed with flying colors. I knew what the issue was but had to rule out the possible physical causes. A week later, after attending Stewart's funeral, I made my 2nd trip to the ER. At that point I realized the ER was not going to do anything for me. I needed to change some things in my life. I had been working 60+ hours and doing almost 40 hours of volunteer work per week. I immediately resigned from the Executive board of the WSRP, my chairmanship of the County GOP, Rob McKenna's and all other campaigns, and told my boss I was not working over 40 hours per week. I took a few days off but found I needed to take meds every night to stop the attacks which were almost daily. My relationship with God got ever stronger, as every night I would pray myself to sleep waiting for the meds to kick in.

Philippians 4:6-7 - Do not be anxious about anything, but in every situation, by prayer and petition, with thanksgiving, present your requests to God. And the peace of God, which transcends all understanding, will guard your hearts and your minds in Christ Jesus.

Matthew 6:34 – Therefore do not worry about tomorrow, for tomorrow will worry about itself.

Eventually things improved though it did come back to haunt me years later. That's the way it was since I got out of the Navy. My days as a political junkie were over…. For now anyway.

2008 brought in the bad with the good, IMHO. President Bush was term limited out and along came Obama. However, Rob won re-election to a 2nd term as Attorney General. That summer, prior to the election, we hosted a fund raising dinner at our house for him, $500 per plate with 15 in attendance. Grace's sister Nancy was here visiting, so I had extra help in the kitchen, and she was a fine Hostess. Grace bartended and Steven valeted cars as the guests arrived.

<u>AG Rob with Grace and me at the head</u>

For the most part I laid low in the political world, with the exception of helping only John Koster in another congressional run and Rob Mc Kenna, when he asked me to Chair his Steering Committee when he announced his run for Governor.

John made his last run for Congress in 2012. To help kick off the campaign, Michael Regan, President Regan's son, was our keynote speaker.

I had listened to Michael for years on the radio and it was a pleasure to meet and spend an evening with him.

John, Michael and me

One day at the State Convention, Rob greeted me with a hug and whispered in my ear that he still had my number. I wasn't sure just what that meant except that he would be calling. Well I got the call and he told me he was going to run for Governor and asked me to Chair his Steering Committee. I told him I was not doing much politically but for him… YES.

You see, back in 2006 when I had to resign all my positions due to the health issues I told you about, Rob, the Attorney General, was the only one that called to check on me, and he did it more than once. About 3 months after those events, he came up to my area and I got a call from his office asking if I was available to have lunch with him. I said of course and asked who else was going to be there. I figured they were putting together some kind of group. I was told nobody, just me and Rob. Well we met at a restaurant in Anacortes and I asked him what did I owe this pleasure to? I told him I'm no longer on the Executive Board, I'm no longer the Chairman, he could have had lunch with anyone. He replied "You are my friend, you helped me and I appreciate that". Well those were the words of a true gentleman, so when he asked me 6 years later to help with the Governor's race I said of course.

Rob arranged for Governor Chris Christie to come to his event to help with his Governor's race

Unfortunately Rob did not get elected. I have my own opinion of what part of the issue was, considering he did so well in both election and re-election for Attorney General. I'm still in touch with Rob and consider him my friend. In the meantime, he is enjoying private law practice probably with much less stress and better pay than public service.

In 2014 Rick was one of three candidates running for county commissioner in our district. He was by far my preferred candidate and I told him if he won the primary to come see me and I would help him in his race. Well he won the primary and I became his campaign manager. We had some good talent helping on the campaign team and Rick was a great candidate, a regular family guy, retired Navy. We won the election by a small margin, 144 votes if I remember correctly. Unfortunately in 2018 when he ran for re-election, his ultra-liberal opponent, who was a well-funded carpetbagger from the Seattle area, was put there to stop the majority Republican County Commissioners.

2019 rolled around and I got an invitation to the Lincoln Day Dinner at a neighboring county. Candice Owens was the keynote speaker. The County Chairwoman, who I did not personally know, knew of my past. She graciously gave me a complimentary pass to the private reception with Candice, and then even sat me at her table for dinner out of respect for my past positions.

Candice is an up and coming star and I hope we see a lot more of her.

I asked Candice to sign a MAGA hat that I was given and inscribe it to my childhood friend Timmy. He loves her but lives in PA so obviously could not be there. He was tickled pink when he got it in the mail.

7.

A Growing Family

I resisted signing up on Facebook for several years but finally gave in and started a page. As much as I hate what FB has become, I am glad I started a page when I did.

One night in June 2012, while on business travel to Orange County, CA, I got a private message on FB. A woman asked me if I had ever been stationed in Jacksonville FL in 1972. I looked at her profile and saw her name which was very unique, and sounded familiar. So I replied back, "Yes I was". It was late in the evening so I then went to bed. The next morning I found another message that said, "Well, I see you are married and I don't want to screw up your life, but you need to know something". And attached was this picture.

Well I was shocked. I looked at Joe's FB page and besides looking like me, and in spite of growing up very differently than I did, we had so much in common. We were both Navy electronics types, both scuba diver, both have boats, and on and on.

My good friend Dr. Cyndee looked at the picture and said "I don't know why you wasted your money on a DNA test, just look at the picture". He was definitely my son.

Joe was 38 at the time I got this message. I asked his mom if Joe knew about me. She said no, so I replied to her that she needed to tell her son. I waited a few days then Joe and I initiated a conversation on FB messenger. Afterwards, we spoke on the phone. This was kind of strange for me and I'm sure for Joe also, but the ice was broken.

When I got home I told Grace about the messages and showed her the picture. At first she did not know how to respond. Keep in mind that I fathered Joe 15 years before I met Grace, so this would not have been much different than if she knew I had a son when we met, except I didn't know yet. That weekend I got a phone call from my 3 newfound grandchildren. Joe was married and had 2 sons and a daughter. The oldest, Aaron, had just graduated high school and Anna was a year younger, and Brandon was a couple of years younger. We had a nice icebreaking conversation.

In November 2012, Grace and I had plans to fly to New York for Thanksgiving. We changed our return flight and flew to Miami first. Joe was living in the Keys, so he drove up to Miami to pick us up at the airport. WOW what an experience meeting for the first time! And guess what? Another thing we had in common was discovered…we both drove a Chevy Silverado. We drove down to the Keys and spent a few days with the new family, helped decorate the Christmas tree, met a couple of their closest friends, shared pictures and stories, and did some sightseeing, since neither of us had been to Key West before. It was a good visit and kickoff for what was going to become a new growing relationship with Joe, Jennifer and the 3 kids.

In April 2013, Dad and Celia had a 50th anniversary party in New York, so Joe and Jennifer flew up to celebrate with us, and start meeting some of the family.

Most of the family had not heard the news yet, so with microphone in hand, I broke the news and made the introduction

    I could just imagine how overwhelmed Joe must have felt meeting all these new cousins at this point in his life, but I know there were all open arms welcoming him and Jen.

    In June of 2013, Anna graduated high school, so we flew down to Miami, rented a car, and drove to the Keys. Denise and Jimmy met us there and we stayed in base lodging at NAS Key West. We got to participate in our granddaughter's graduation ceremony, which was very special for us. Since Joe and Jen were both turning 40 that year, we gifted them 2 airline tickets to join us at our timeshare in Kona the following January 2014.

    Independence Day week, Joe, Jen and the three kids flew up to New York so they could all meet more of their new family. Cousins Gina and Alex graciously allowed us to have a party at their house, since they had a large yard and pool. We hired servers and a cleanup crew so everyone could spend as much quality time as possible with each other. We had over 100 cousins, aunts and uncles attend. I can't imagine how overwhelmed Joe, Jen and the kids must have been meeting so many new cousins that they never knew they had. The weather was perfect, and like all Italian events, the food was plentiful and yummy.

**Left to Right
Grace, Anna, Andy, Denise, Jim, Dad, Celia, Aaron, Jen, Joe and Brandon**

Since this was the kid's first trip to the Big Apple, we tried to cram in as many sights and experiences as possible. We took them to Little Italy so they could explore the delis, pastry shops and, of course, real pizza.

No trip to New York would be complete without a ride on the subway. Heading downtown on the Pelham Bay #6 train (same one as "Taking of Pelham 123" movie)

We did as much as anyone could fit into one day. Unfortunately, the weather was a little wet and the rain ponchos came off and on a dozen times that day as we toured Manhattan.

Ground Zero

Our visitors were well worn out by the end of the day!

In January 2014, Joe and Jen flew to Seattle to meet up with us to go to Hawaii. I picked them up at the airport and they came home with us for a day or two before we all departed to the airport to catch our flight to Kona. We had an AWESOME time together and did some new things in Kona that Grace and I had not done in the 20 years we have been going there.

We got to see lots of whales as that is the time of year that the humpbacks are plentiful.

We went on a flume ride, whale watching, fine dining, horseback riding, fishing, drove to tour the Volcano, and of course a little shopping. Joe rented a board and caught a few waves.

Grace's favorite was horseback riding (lol). We all had Hawaiian named horses except Grace's was named Charlie

In January 2015, the front door bell rang in the late morning. I opened the door to find my grandson Brandon, who said to me, "My parents threw me out, can I stay here?". And then suddenly, Joe and Jen appeared from the bushes. They had flown in from Key West to surprise me for my 60th birthday. It was well planned and coordinated with Grace. What a great surprise and awesome gift for me!

This was a first trip to the area for Brandon and also, having grown up in Guam and Key West, his first time in snow country, so we took a ride up to Mount Baker.

Brandon's first time experience making a snow angel or feeling the impact of a snowball! We had a great tour of the mountain, and it also gave Joe a reminder of driving on snow, since he left Maine years ago.

My 60th birthday party was well attended at a local restaurant in town, with the addition of our nephew Eric, who also flew in from SoCal for the occasion.

Later that spring I made a trip down to the Keys to visit my son and family. We got to have lots of private time in the kitchen, at the dining table, the living room, out on the boat, the local taverns and streets of Key West. Brandon was home at that time so I got to hang with him also. Then Anna gave a surprise visit when she flew in for a Detachment from NAS Lemoore, CA. I got to go have a few drinks with her and her shipmates. I cherish our time together.

Joe and I went out on his boat. The waters in the Keys are much different than the Pacific Northwest where we live. Most of the inshore waters are quite shallow, maybe 20 feet or so. The beaches are sandy, which makes for some good places to either anchor or beach your boat, and enjoy some semi-secluded areas that are only accessible by water. "Snipes" is a common place to meet and hang out with other boaters and friends.

Boating with the local friends and family

I got a very pleasant surprise from my granddaughter in July 2015 when she told me she was going to take some leave and come up to visit. WOW she made her grandfather so happy! This was great bonding time for us since it was just Anna, Grace and me.

My beautiful granddaughter on the top of Mount Erie and on the boat waiting for the crabs to run into the traps. NO she does not smoke cigars. This was sent to her mother saying "Look, grandpa has me smoking cigars" as a joke. I was so happy she came to visit and hope we can do it again.

In November, Denise and Jim, Joe and Jen, Grace and I took a cruise. This was a Caribbean cruise with ports including Jamaica, Mexico and Grand Cayman. Celebrity was a great cruise line and we had a good time. It was Jennifer's birthday so we celebrated on the ship.

Joe sitting with Pop in the BIG chair on deck, just chillin

It was a fun cruise and did well on the craps table, lol.

OPUS DINING ROOM
Celebrity Reflection

After the cruise ship returned to Ft. Lauderdale, we flew up to spend a week with Sandra in Pensacola. She drove us to New Orleans from where we flew home.

Brandon didn't have any big plans for the summer of '16, so we flew him out to stay with us for a while. I mentioned to him that I was going to need help replacing the roof on our rental house, but as it turned out, a higher priority project came up. When the tenants moved out they left a nightmare behind. Evidently there was a leak in the bathroom sink that they never told me about so it dripped for many months. As a result, it rotted the subfloor in the bathroom and laundry room. So Brandon was about to get his first lesson on carpentry.

Brandon proved to be a hard working carpenter apprentice. He learned how to rip out the old section of flooring, put in new joists, sub flooring and finish flooring,

I wished he lived closer as there is so much that grandpa could teach him to do. I never really had that chance growing up, but I did get the experience in the various jobs I had in life. It would be nice to be able to pass down your knowledge and plant the seeds for memories that will last a lifetime for them.

We would have liked to have spent time on the boat doing some crabbing and just hanging out, but unfortunately, it was in the shop. Brandon is an avid boater having spent much of his growing years in the Keys. Next time!

So instead, I took him to the local gun club and let him experience some learning in gun safety.

We had a blast and Brandon got to experience something he doesn't get to do at home

We went to the antique car show in town and looked at all the old muscle cars and wished. Also the Swinomish Casino had their seafood buffet and an outside movie.

Now here is a happy camper, all the Dungeness crab you can eat at the buffet! Not sure they made any profit on us that night

Then in the summer of '17, Brandon came back out again to do everything that we didn't get to do his last trip. Since he now had his driver's license so he was able to get around with our extra vehicle. He did help me with a couple of repairs on my pickup that I was not too motivated to do. This trip we got to get out on the boat too!

1st Mate Brandon at the helm   **A couple of monsters**

This year we got to do the roof that we didn't do last year. I thought this would be a good learning experience for Brandon, possibly open the opportunity for a part time side job, or at least be able to do his own house someday.

He did a great job for a first time roofer, though he said it sucked and never wanted to do another!

And as a thank you for helping me, Brandon wanted really badly to eat at the Seattle Space Needle. We made a reservation for brunch and made his day.

Just by coincidence, when we got done eating and went to the stairs that go to the rest rooms, I ran into a friend named Cindy. She was a cop in Huntington Beach that used to have breakfast at the local establishment on Main Street, the "Sugar Shack". She had been on an Alaska cruise with her granddaughter and was heading home after her ship pulled back into the port of Seattle. It is certainly a small world!

In December '18, we took a trip to visit Sandra in Pensacola and borrowed her car to drive to Jacksonville where we met up with Joe, Jen, Aaron and Brandon in Anna's apartment. We had a nice visit. One thing that impressed me was Anna pulling out a big storage box where she kept her mementos. It was nice to see that there were things in her past that she held on to. That gave me hope that someday Grace and I would be in that box too.

Three Generations of men   **4 Generations of Service**

8.

Friends, Old and New

As I mentioned before, I am not a big Facebook fan. I think Zucker is a socialist that is hurting our country, our society and our children. When it first started, it was a place where everyone shared pictures of their dinner and pork chop recipes. It has grown to be a place that fosters hatred, bias, censorship, and destruction of certain people's lives who have differing views.

However there still is a positive side to it. Over the years, in addition to discovering my son Joe, it also helped me to reconnect with some old childhood friends as well as to keep in touch with other friends and family. Let's face it, nobody is going to write letters any longer. Heck, even email is becoming a thing of the past along with telephone voice conversations. The only exception may be from the guy that wants to sell you an extended warrantee on the car that you may not even own anymore.

Some people I know have no desire or drive to keep in touch with people from their past, no less reconnecting with them. I, on the other hand, am not like that. I find it stimulating and exciting to reconnect with childhood friends and have conversations with them catching up on the past few decades. Just by joining a FB group on Syosset High School, I actually have reconnected with several people and that I maybe even be closer friends now than before. Part of this phenomenon may be because of mutual friends that we are close with, that then brings you closer to them. It's somewhat similar to the family matriarch that is the glue of the family while they are still alive. Our mutual friend Lori, who wrote to me every week when I was deployed to South East Asia, was instrumental in meeting for dinner with Denise, who did not remember what a crush I had on her back then. On a recent trip back to New York, I had dinner with Carol, who was more of an acquaintance in high school. We keep in touch on FB now. Lori and I continue to stay in close touch and she is my BFF.

Lori and me c.1975   Lori, me and Denise c.2016

She put me up for a week or so when I went back to visit with my dad before he died.

Of course this brings into light another reality of life. You start to become more aware of friends you grew up with that have bigger life issues than you do, and also those that may be dying or have died already. It brings awareness to your own mortality, as you start searching for people from your past, only to find out that they have died 10 or even 20 years ago.

I found my 6th grade class picture and posted it on FB on my grade school's group page. It resulted in 184 comments, 28 likes and 3 shares. WOW! 184 comments. In looking through them I found several classmates that I had not seen or heard from since '69. Even children of my classmates connected with me. I found this to be fun and very interesting. That is also how I found out that the teacher I had in 6th and 8th grade had been charged with being a pedophile and that he was now dead.

I also reconnected with some of the people I grew up with in the 60s from the old neighborhood in The Bronx. I found Dale Anne, who then connected me with her brother Tim, who uses an incognito name on FB. Tim and I were friends when I was young in spite of him being about 5 years older than me, like a big brother. He is a musician and we used to hang out on the stoop and jam with our guitars. Since reconnecting, I have gotten together with Dale Anne, Tim and his lovely wife when I was back in New York.

Janine, Tim, me and Dale Anne c.2018

Now we call each other on the phone (yup, the old fashioned way) a couple of times a month. Tim gave me a New Testament when I joined the Navy, and inscribed it to me in 1971. I still have it 50 years later, and recently sent him a picture of it which made surprised him greatly. Since Tim a minister's son, we have had numerous religious and philosophical conversations on many topics. He is an important reconnection in my life now, and I still feel that big brother (the real big brother not the government) connection with him.

I must also tell you about Mike, aka Burger. As I mentioned earlier, Mike was the other big brother in the neighborhood. He was in the age group that Timmy was in, a few years older than me. Mike took me to the recruiter and guided me in signing up for the Navy, having just completed his own enlistment in the Army. We lost touch since about 1980 but were able to reconnect when I got his phone number through a trail of friends. We have since been able to visit when he and his wife Neli returned from an Alaska cruise to Seattle. I picked them up when their ship pulled in, and they spent a few days with us.

c. 2017

A great visit after nearly 40 years. Mike, Neli, Grace with Romeo and me. Looking forward to another visit after all the Covid problems in this country are resolved

Bobby and Ralph are my 2 lifelong friends from the block growing up. We are the same age group and have known each other since 1962. I went back to the old neighborhood in April 2013 to see what the block looked like. Joe was in New York for my dad's 50th, so he got to meet 2 of my old friends and see the block and neighborhood I grew up in.

c.2013
Ralph and Bobby. We are still in touch after 59 years of friendship. Ralph still lives on the block and Bobby is in Illinois.

We shared many high school dances, many six packs of beers, many problems and life stories with each other. Bobby's sister's boyfriend Greg, now her husband, used to take us surfing to Gilgo Beach, on Long Island when we were teenagers. He had a very cool 1966 GTO convertible. It was a blast driving to the beach with the board in the car and the top down.

Now I am looking forward to a face to face get-together with some of the old friends I have reconnected with online over the past couple of years that I have not seen since '69 or '70. My next few trips to New York will be busy and I think very enjoyable.

I was also able to reconnect with some old shipmates from my years in the Navy. As I mentioned earlier, Garrel Powers was killed in an accident on the flight deck of the U.S.S. Kitty hawk, but I bumped into another Garrel Powers who turned out to be his son. Several others, around a dozen or so, and a new one pops up every once in the while.

I also met a Seminarian who lives in Uganda named Derrick. Brother Derrick reached out to me with a friend request which I accepted. We have chatted regularly since last year and even had voice calls which you can now do for free with apps such as Facebook. He joined me and some Brother Knights in our daily Rosary group that we do online on occasion and became interested in the Knights of Columbus, so I happily sponsored him and he is now a 3rd degree Knight.

 A good young man who will be a fine priest someday.

And I must mention my dear friend Miko. Back around 2005, I got a chat message on Skype ... Hello. So I asked, hello do I know you? She replied "oh I'm sorry if I am bothering you". I told her it was no bother. She lived in Xiamen China and was about 24 years old and was studying English, and was looking for someone to practice with. We chatted 4 to 5 days a week for years. She was there for me more than once late at night when I needed someone. She also confided in me many times about things in her life. Though we have not met face to face, we remain good friends. She has since gotten married and had 2 children, the first born who she named Andy (his English name)! Now that he is growing up, on occasion he sends "Uncle Andy" a message when his mom is online with me. I pray that someday we get to meet

F2F. Hopefully she will be able to visit the U.S. because it's a bit longer trip than I may want to make again at this point in my life.

Miko age 24 when we met   Baby Andy age 5

We have been blessed with a number of newer friends since moving away from New York. I made a few close friends in SoCal while on all the business trips I mentioned earlier. There are Steve and Marina, John Kelly, my dear Dr. Cyndee, and JC from The Winery. Here on Whidbey we met our very good friend Sandra who unfortunately moved back to Pensacola, Donna and Fred who moved to Spokane, Bill and Renee, who decided they liked us so much they bought the lot across the street from us to build THEIR retirement home on. There are also Barry and Roberta, Helen and Jim, Dan and Ginger, and the list goes on.

My career at Boeing brought into our lives Shahab and Sahar, Bill and Chikako, Andy, Maddy, Diego and Denise, Cindy and Fred, Dave and Bridget.

Then there are my Brother Knights (Knights of Columbus), some that I have known for many years and some that are newer friends, including the Knights in Hawaii.

Obviously I could not go on to list every single one, but these are some of the closer friends that we stay in touch with regularly. My point here is to share that we have been blessed with many friendships.

Credits

Thank you to all that motivated me and suggested I should write this book.

Thank you to all those that are in this book because you are part of the many blessings of my life.

Thank you to my sister-in-law Nancy, who painstakingly, word by word, sentence by sentence, helped me edit this book.

Memories

Jacqueline Benedetto, mom, RIP

Andrew Valrosa, dad, RIP

Denise Valrosa Albertelli, sister, RIP

Barry, aka Bear, friend & shipmate, RIP

CPSIA information can be obtained
at www.ICGtesting.com
Printed in the USA
BVHW091141230922
647764BV00023BA/1346